The DANIEL

FAST

COOKBOOK

DELICIOUS AND

NUTRITIOUS RECIPES

FOR A 21-DAY FAST

Graham Feola

D1282519

CHAPTER THREE

[Soups and Salads: Recipes for hearty soups, light salads, and other nourishing dishes that are perfect for lunch or dinner.]

CHAPTER FOUR

[Main Courses: Recipes for plant-based proteins, grains, and vegetables that is sure to satisfy your hunger and your taste buds.]

CHAPTER FIVE

CHAPTER SIX

INTRODUCTION

FASTING EXPLAINED

Fasting was designed by God, not to change Him, but rather to change us! Fasting doesn't show God that you are good or deserving. Only Jesus Christ does that for us. However, fasting does bring us into an experience where our hearts are more open to what the Lord wants to show us for our individual lives.

Fasting safely and appropriately is one of the ways the Bible encourages believers to connect with and grow closer to God. It increases dependence on the power of the Spirit, and proves that man does not live on bread alone.

TYPES OF FASTS

When most people think of fasting the first image that usually comes to the mind of a person is going without food for several days and drinking only water, broth and

Juice. Although fasting comes in a variety of forms, there are basically four types:

- Absolute
- Supernatural absolute
- Liquid
- Partial

An **absolute fast** is a fast form is the fast from all food and liquids for a few days, which is what the Apostle Paul experience after the Lord appeared to him on the road to Damascus (Acts 9-9). Another example is when Queen Esther sent a message through Mordecai asking the Jews to fast with her before she went to see the King. She said, do not eat or drink for 3 days (Esther 4:16).

A **supernatural absolute fast** requires refraining from eating and drinking for a greater period of time than the absolute fast. It is referred to as supernatural because the length of time involved is medically impossible to survive without the Divine empowerment of the Holy Spirit, such as when Moses was without food or water for forty days on Mount Sinai when he received the Ten Commandments from the Lord (Exodus 34:28).

A **liquid fast** involves eliminating food for some time and consuming only water, fruit juices, and vegetable juices. The Bible does not mention a liquid fast specifically, but it's an option that many people choose especially when fasting for more than two or three days. This type of fast is not quite as taxing on the body as an absolute fast, and there is typically no danger of dehydration if the adequate liquid is consumed.

On a **partial fast**, certain foods are removed from the diet for a specific length of time. The prophet Daniel chose to undergo a partial fast when he sought the Lord. His fasting experiences form the basis of the Daniel Fast.

HOW THIS BOOK WILL HELP YOU

Once you decide to do the Daniel Fast, it's important that you understand what your commitment involves. You certainly don't want to jump into your fast without first considering the time, attention, and energy you will need to invest in it. Your first step is to formulate a plan. Without some kind of structure, you will more than likely struggle with frustration and discouragement. The Daniel Fast Cookbook is your plan of action and your toolbox. It is divided into three parts consisting of nine chapters:

PART 1, which consist of chapter 1, explains what the Daniel Fast is, gives the biblical basis for the guide- lines of the fast, outlines the benefits of the Daniel Fast, looks at what types of foods should be consumed during the fast and what shouldn't, and helps you create your fasting plan.

PART 2, which consists of chapters 2-6, addresses the physical aspect of the Daniel Fast. It identifies the foods to eat and the foods to avoid, as well as provides over twenty tasty and nutritious recipes that are easy to prepare. This section also contains a suggested one-week meal plan, suggested grocery and pantry list for your shopping, which will provide direction and show you how to organize the food component of your fast.

PART 3, consisting of chapters 7-9, delve into the spiritual component of your twenty-one-day adventure with the Lord, which is the reason you are fasting in the first place. You're sacrificing what you want physically because you're hungry for more of God. You have a desire to discern what he wants to accomplish in and through your life. This section of the book features twenty-one thought-provoking scripture readings that will strengthen your faith as you fix your eyes on Jesus.

The journey on which you are about to embark is an exciting one. My prayer for you is that you will know the Lord more intimately as a result of your Daniel Fast experience and that you will be "filled to the measure of all the fullness of God" (Eph. 3:19).

Think of this book as a companion who will accompany you along the way. When you want ideas on what to cook for dinner, you can quickly and easily find a recipe. When you feel weary, you can be refreshed through Bible verses and devotions. When you are struggling with staying committed, you can refer to the information and tools in this book to motivate you.

So whether you're a seasoned faster or a beginner, whether you're looking to lose weight, improve your health, or simply grow closer to God, we hope that this cookbook will be a helpful resource as you undertake the Daniel Fast. May it inspire and equip you to make the most of this special time of fasting and prayer, and may it help you experience the physical, emotional, and spiritual benefits that come from this time of discipline and devotion.

CHAPTER ONE

[Introduction to the Daniel Fast: What it is, why it's done, and how to customize it to your individual needs and goals.]

WHAT IS THE DANIEL FAST?

Definition Of The Daniel Fast

The Daniel Fast is a spiritual discipline that involves abstaining from certain foods and focusing on prayer and Bible study for a period of 21 days. Based on the account of the prophet Daniel in the Old Testament, the Daniel Fast is a partial fast that allows for the consumption of fruits, vegetables, whole grains, legumes, and water. It is often undertaken for the purpose of seeking a closer relationship with God, improving physical health, or addressing specific areas of personal or spiritual growth.

The Daniel Fast is an opportunity to draw closer to God and to make positive changes in your life. It's a chance to press pause on the distractions of the world and to focus on what really matters: your relationship with God and the health of your body.

Participating in a Daniel Fast requires eliminating commonly enjoyed foods for twenty-one days as an act of worship and of consecrating oneself to God. Foods that are allowed are fruits, vegetables, whole grains, legumes, nuts, seeds, and oils. Restricted foods include dairy, meat, sugar, all forms of sweeteners, yeast, refined and processed foods, deep-fried foods, and solid fats.

You don't have to be a spiritual giant to do a Daniel Fast. It's for anyone who is hungry for a deeper connection with the Lord and who is also willing to make a three-week commitment to the spiritual discipline of fasting as a means of pursuing that connection. Because it is a partial fast, as opposed to an absolute or liquid fast, participants are able to eat a wide variety of foods. For this reason, the Daniel Fast is a good entry-level fast. However, if you have a medical condition or any health concerns, you should consult with your physician before beginning any type of fast, including the Daniel Fast.

The guidelines of the modern-day Daniel Fast are based on the fasting experiences of the prophet Daniel. We follow his example not so much because his diet is worth emulating as because his heart is worth emulating. In the book of Daniel, chapters 1 and 10, we discover how Daniel's passion for God caused him to long for spiritual food more than physical food, which is the ultimate desire of anyone choosing to participate in a fast. As we take a closer look at what he did, it's important to remember that we're not trying to duplicate Daniel's menu, but we do want to imitate the spirit in which he fasted.

History And Biblical Basis Of The Daniel Fast

The book of Daniel tells the story of the Israelites carried off into exile after many years of straying from God's ways, but mostly from the perspective of a handful of individuals. It also contains prophecy.

Daniel was one of the youths selected to be educated in the ways of the Babylonian court, the center of the Chaldean empire. He learned literature, another language, court etiquette, and many other skills that would make him useful to Nebuchadnezzar. Daniel's diet first comes up in chapter one of the accounts of his life:

"But Daniel resolved that he would not defile himself with the king's food, or with the wine that he drank. Therefore he asked the chief of the eunuchs to allow him not to defile himself" (Daniel 1:8).

Centuries before, God instituted rules for which foods were clean and unclean for Hebrews to eat, which the Chaldeans did not know or obey.

There are two important factors that went into Daniel's request to eat differently than everyone else in his cohort. First and foremost, he wanted to continue to obey the Lord's commands. Throughout the course of the book of Daniel, his dedication to the Lord is clear. He prays even under threat of death. He boldly interprets prophecy under the guidance of the Spirit of God, knowing it could anger the king.

Keeping his diet was part of being obedient to God. It was also important because it was a part of maintaining his identity as an Israelite. Being chosen for service in the court of Nebuchadnezzar cost the Hebrew men a great deal, even their own names. The Bible records, "And the chief of the eunuchs gave them names: Daniel he called Belteshazzar, Hananiah he called Shadrach, Mishael he called Meschach, and Azariah he called Abednego" (Daniel 1:7). They were no longer in their homes, had to learn a new language, lived as well-dressed and well-fed prisoners, but they had to go by new names. Daniel clung to his identity and his God, in part by eating cleanly.

The chief eunuch had compassion on Daniel and his request to eat according to his principles, but he had concerns that the king would get mad when Daniel and his friends were less healthy because they were not eating approved food. As a response, Daniel gave a challenge to the Babylonian court. He said: "Test your servants for ten days; let us be given vegetables to eat and water to drink. Then let our appearance and the appearance of the youths who eat the king's food be observed by you, and deal with your servants according to what you see" (Daniel 1:13-14).

The king's men still ate meat and wine, and were less healthy than Daniel and his friends. Today, believers will sometimes adopt this diet to get healthier and to get closer to the Lord, as they often incorporate a fast with it. In the Bible it lasted for ten days initially, and then it was implemented for a longer period of time.

Benefits Of The Daniel Fast

The Daniel Fast is more than just a diet or a detox program; it is a spiritual discipline that can bring numerous physical, mental, emotional, and spiritual benefits to your life. By following the Daniel Fast, you can improve your health, your energy, your mood, and your relationships, and you can experience a closer and deeper connection with God.

Here are some of the benefits of the Daniel Fast:

- **Physical benefits:** The Daniel Fast can help you to improve your physical health, by providing you with a balanced and nutritious diet, that is rich in fiber, vitamins, minerals, and antioxidants, and that is low in saturated fat, cholesterol, and additives. By eating a variety of whole foods, such as fruits, vegetables, whole grains, legumes, nuts, and seeds, you can boost your immune system, your digestion, your metabolism, and your energy levels, and you can reduce your risk of chronic diseases, such as diabetes, heart disease, and cancer.
- **Mental benefits**: The Daniel Fast can also help you to improve your mental health, by reducing your stress, your anxiety, and your depression, and by increasing your focus, your concentration, and your

memory. By eliminating or minimizing your intake of caffeine, sugar, and other stimulants, you can reduce your reliance on these substances, and you can improve your sleep quality and duration, and you can enhance your overall cognitive function.

- **Emotional benefits:** The Daniel Fast can enhance your emotional health, by increasing your joy, your peace, and your gratitude, and by decreasing your anger, your frustration, and your resentment. By committing to the Daniel Fast, you can set aside your own desires and preferences, and you can focus on God's will and His blessings, and you can cultivate a more positive and optimistic attitude towards life.

- **Spiritual benefits:** The Daniel Fast can deepen your spiritual health, by strengthening your faith, your trust, and your obedience, and by increasing your intimacy, your fellowship, and your worship. By fasting and praying, you can draw closer to God, and you can surrender your life to Him, and you can experience His presence and His guidance in a more profound and personal way.

WHAT CAN YOU EAT ON THE DANIEL FAST?

The Daniel fast is a partial fast, meaning it does not require the individual to give up all food for a period of time, though some people will abstain from eating before dinner. It is very strict about what foods can be consumed. The Bible does not go into great detail about what specifically he ate, though it does say Daniel and his friends consumed vegetables and water. The Daniel fast is built around this knowledge, an understanding of Levitical law, and clean foods.

Foods That Are Allowed On The Daniel Fast

- Vegetables: all fresh, frozen, dried, juiced, and canned vegetables

- Fruit: all fresh, frozen, dried (with no added sugar), juiced and canned fruit

- Whole grains: amaranth, barley, brown rice, buckwheat, bulgur, millet. Freekeh, oats, purple rice, wild rice, whole wheat, spelt, rye, quinoa

- Beans and legumes: black beans, garbanzo beans, kidney beans, lentils, peanuts, pinto beans, split beans, black-eyed peas

- Oils: coconut, olive, sesame, etc., but not for deep-frying

- Nuts and seeds: almonds, Brazil nuts, cashews, sunflower seeds, soy nuts, sesame seeds, hazelnuts, macadamia nuts, pecans, pumpkin seeds, pine nuts, pistachios, poppy seeds

- Unleavened bread, herbs, spices, and seasonings

- Beverages: water, some fruit juice, unsweetened non-dairy milk

Foods That Are Not Allowed On The Daniel Fast

- Alcohol

- Added sugars: any foods with added sugar are prohibited, agave, artificial sweeteners, brown sugar, cane juice, corn syrup, honey, sugar, molasses, etc.

- Meat: beef, bison, chicken, goat, lamb, pork, turkey, fish

- Dairy: butter, cheese, cream, milk, yogurt

- Eggs are prohibited

- Yeast: this includes all leavened bread

- Refined grains: white rice, white flour

- Processed food: any food with artificial flavorings, colorings, chemicals, additives, and preservatives are prohibited

- Fried food: corn chips, potato chips, French fries, fried vegetables (tempura) etc.

- Solid fats: butter, lard, margarine, shortening

- Chocolate: milk chocolate, semi-sweet, dark, syrup, cacao

- Caffeinated drinks

HOW TO CUSTOMIZE THE DANIEL FAST TO YOUR INDIVIDUAL NEEDS AND GOALS

The Daniel Fast can be customized to your individual needs and goals. If you have specific dietary preferences or medical conditions, you can adapt the fast to meet your needs. For example, if you are a vegetarian or vegan, you can focus on plant-based proteins like beans and tofu. If you are lactose intolerant, you can opt for plant-based milks like almond milk or coconut milk.

Tips For Adapting The Daniel Fast To Your Personal Preferences And Dietary Needs

The Daniel Fast is a flexible and adaptable spiritual discipline that can be customized and personalized to fit your unique preferences and dietary needs. By adapting the Daniel Fast to your personal preferences and dietary needs, you can make the fast more enjoyable, more sustainable, and more beneficial, and you can avoid the frustration, the disappointment, and the temptation to quit.

Here are some tips for adapting the Daniel Fast to your personal preferences and dietary needs:

- **Consult with your healthcare provider:** To adapt the Daniel Fast to your personal preferences and dietary needs, you can consult with your healthcare provider, and you can discuss your goals, your concerns, and your medical history and you can receive guidance and recommendations. Your healthcare provider can help you to determine if the Daniel Fast is appropriate for you, and if there are any adjustments or modifications that you need to make, based on your health status, your medications, or your allergies. By consulting with your healthcare provider, you can ensure that the Daniel Fast is safe and healthy for you, and you can avoid potential risks or complications.

- **Customize your meals and your snacks:** To adapt the Daniel Fast to your personal preferences and dietary needs, you can customize your meals and your snacks, and you can choose the foods and the ingredients that you enjoy, and that are compatible with your preferences and your needs. You can customize your meals and your snacks by using different spices and herbs, by adding or substituting ingredients, by trying different recipes and cooking techniques, or by adjusting the portion sizes and the frequency of your meals. By customizing your meals and your snacks, you can make the fast more appealing and satisfying, and you can avoid boredom or dissatisfaction, and you can stay motivated and committed to the fast.

- **Seek support and resources:** To adapt the Daniel Fast to your personal preferences and dietary needs, you can seek support and resources, and you can find resources and tips online, or you can ask for help and advice from others who have completed the Daniel Fast, or who have experience in nutrition or cooking. You can seek support and resources by joining a support group or a accountability group, by finding a accountability partner or a accountability coach, by participating in a community event or a service project, or by joining a church or a ministry. By seeking support and resources, you can receive encouragement and guidance, and you can learn from others, and you can adapt the Daniel Fast to your personal preferences and dietary needs more effectively and efficiently.

- **Experiment and learn:** To adapt the Daniel Fast to your personal preferences and dietary needs, you can experiment and learn, and you can try different foods and recipes, and you can observe and record your reactions and your progress, and you can adjust your meals and your snacks accordingly. You can experiment and learn by keeping a food diary or a journal, by tracking your energy and your mood, by measuring your weight and your vital signs, or by taking photos and videos of your meals and your snacks. By experimenting and learning, you can discover what works and what doesn't work for you, and you can tailor the Daniel Fast to your personal preferences and dietary needs, and you can optimize your health and your well-being.

- **Be flexible and open-minded:** To adapt the Daniel Fast to your personal preferences and dietary needs, you can be flexible and open-minded, and you can be willing to change and to try new things, and you can be patient and understanding with yourself, and you can let go of perfectionism or judgment. You can be flexible and open-minded by accepting that the Daniel Fast is a journey, and not a destination, and by recognizing that the fast may have ups and downs, twists and turns, and by learning from your mistakes and your challenges, and by celebrating your achievements and your growth. By being flexible and open-minded, you can adapt the Daniel Fast to your personal preferences and dietary needs more easily and more gracefully, and you can enjoy the process and the benefits of the fast, more fully and more deeply.

Ideas for Setting Specific Goals and Intentions for Your Daniel Fast

Setting specific goals and intentions for your Daniel Fast can help you to focus and to clarify your purpose, and it can motivate and inspire you to make the most of your fast, and to achieve your desired outcomes. By setting specific goals and intentions for your Daniel Fast, you can make your fast more meaningful and more purposeful, and you can make it more rewarding and more fulfilling, and you can make it more aligned with your values and your vision.

Here are some ideas for setting specific goals and intentions for your Daniel Fast:

- **Identify your values and your vision:** To set specific goals and intentions for your Daniel Fast, you can identify your values and your vision, and you can reflect on what is most important and most meaningful to you, and you can pray and ask God to reveal His will and His purpose for your fast. Your values and your vision can be personal or communal, and they can be spiritual or practical, and they can be related to your health, your relationships, your work, or your ministry. By identifying your values and your vision, you can set goals and intentions that are aligned with your deepest and most authentic desires, and you can make your fast more purposeful and more meaningful.

- **Determine your priorities and your goals**: To set specific goals and intentions for your Daniel Fast, you can determine your priorities and your goals, and you can assess your current situation and your desired outcomes, and you can set specific, measurable, achievable, relevant, and time-bound (SMART) goals. Your priorities and your goals can be related to your physical, emotional, mental, or spiritual health, and they can be specific or general, and they can be short-term or long-term, and they can be realistic or ambitious. By determining your priorities and your goals, you can set goals and intentions that are realistic and achievable, and you can make your fast more effective and more efficient, and you can make it more rewarding and more fulfilling.

- **Create a plan and a schedule:** To set specific goals and intentions for your Daniel Fast, you can create a plan and a schedule, and you can outline the steps and the activities that you need to take and to complete, and you can allocate the time and the resources that you need to achieve your goals. Your plan and your schedule can be as simple or as detailed as you need, and they can be flexible or rigid

- **Review and adjust your plan and your schedule:** To set specific goals and intentions for your Daniel Fast, you can review and adjust your plan and your schedule, and you can assess your progress and your challenges, and you can make changes or adjustments as needed. You can review and adjust your plan and your schedule by tracking your food intake, your exercise, your sleep, your stress, and your relationships, and by comparing your actual performance to your goals and your schedule. By reviewing and adjusting your plan and your schedule, you can make your fast more efficient and more effective, and you can stay on track and avoid distractions or setbacks, and you can make your fast more rewarding and more fulfilling.

- **Seek support and accountability:** To set specific goals and intentions for your Daniel Fast, you can seek support and accountability, and you can enlist the help and the encouragement of others, and you can share your goals and your challenges, and you can hold each other accountable and responsible. You can seek support and accountability by joining a support group or a accountability group, by finding a accountability partner or a accountability coach, by participating in a community event or a service project, or by joining a church or a ministry. By seeking support and accountability, you can avoid isolation and loneliness, and you can benefit from the wisdom and the experience of others, and you can stay motivated and accountable, and you can make your fast more enjoyable and more sustainable.

- **Reflect and evaluate:** To set specific goals and intentions for your Daniel Fast, you can reflect and evaluate, and you can review your progress and your experiences, and you can assess your achievements and your challenges, and you can learn from your fast. You can reflect and evaluate by keeping a journal or a diary, by tracking your food intake, your exercise, your sleep, your stress, and your relationships, or by completing a self-assessment or a feedback form. By reflecting and evaluating, you can identify your strengths and your weaknesses, and you can learn from your successes and your mistakes, and you can set better and more realistic goals and intentions for your next fast, and you can make your fast more meaningful and more purposeful.

Suggestions for Seeking Guidance and Support from Others (E.G., Pastor, Mentor, Accountability Partner)

Seeking guidance and support from others during the Daniel Fast can be beneficial and helpful, as it can provide you with encouragement, accountability, and resources and it can help you to overcome challenges and to stay motivated and committed to the fast. By seeking guidance and support from others during the Daniel Fast, you can make the fast more enjoyable and more sustainable, and you can make it more meaningful and more purposeful, and you can make it more aligned with your values and your vision.

Here are some suggestions for seeking guidance and support from others during the Daniel Fast:

- **Join a support group or a accountability group:** To seek guidance and support from others during the Daniel Fast, you can join a support group or a accountability group, and you can find a group that is dedicated to the Daniel Fast, or that is interested in fasting or in spiritual growth, and you can participate in the group's activities and discussions,

and you can share your experiences and your
challenges, and you can receive feedback and
support. You can join a support group or a
accountability group by contacting your church or
your ministry, by searching online or through social
media, by asking for recommendations from friends
or from your healthcare provider, or by attending a
community event or a service project. By joining a
support group or a accountability group, you can
benefit from the wisdom and the experience of
others, and you can receive encouragement and
accountability, and you can make your fast more
enjoyable and more sustainable.

- **Find a accountability partner or a accountability
  coach:** To seek guidance and support from others
  during the Daniel Fast, you can find a
  accountability partner or a accountability coach,
  and you can connect with someone who has
  completed the Daniel Fast, or who has experience
  in fasting or in spiritual growth, and you can
  schedule regular meetings or phone calls, and you
  can discuss your goals and your challenges, and you
  can offer feedback and support to each other. You
  can find a accountability partner or a accountability
  coach by contacting your church or your ministry,
  by searching online or through social media, by

asking for recommendations from friends or from your healthcare provider, or by attending a community event or a service project. By finding a accountability partner or a accountability coach, you can receive personalized guidance and support, and you can stay motivated and accountable, and you can make your fast more meaningful and more purposeful.

- **Participate in a community event or a service project:** To seek guidance and support from others during the Daniel Fast, you can participate in a community event or a service project, and you can find an event or a project that is related to the Daniel Fast, or that is consistent with your values and your vision, and you can volunteer your time and your skills, and you can interact with others, and you can learn and grow. You can participate in a community event or a service project by contacting your church or your ministry, by searching online or through social media, by asking for recommendations from friends or from your healthcare provider, or by attending a community event or a service project. By participating in a community event or a service project, you can contribute to a cause or a need, and you can learn and grow, and you can make your fast more meaningful and more purposeful, and you can make a difference in the world.

- **Seek guidance and support from a healthcare provider:** To seek guidance and support from others during the Daniel Fast, you can seek guidance and support from a healthcare provider, and you can consult with a healthcare provider who is familiar with the Daniel Fast, or who has experience in fasting or in nutrition, and you can discuss your goals and your challenges, and you can receive feedback and support. You can seek guidance and support from a healthcare provider by contacting your healthcare provider, by searching online or through social media, by asking for recommendations from friends or from your support group or accountability group, or by attending a healthcare event or a seminar. By seeking guidance and support from a healthcare provider, you can receive professional guidance and support, and you can optimize your health and your well-being, and you can make your fast more effective and more efficient, and you can reduce the risk of adverse effects.

- **Seek guidance and support from a pastor or a mentor:** To seek guidance and support from others during the Daniel Fast, you can seek guidance and support from a pastor or a mentor, and you can consult with a pastor or a mentor who is familiar with the Daniel Fast, or who has experience in fasting or in spiritual growth, and you can discuss your goals and your challenges, and you can receive feedback and support. You can seek guidance and support from a pastor or a mentor by contacting your church or your ministry, by searching online or through social media, by asking for recommendations from friends or from your support group or accountability group, or by attending a church service or a spiritual retreat. By seeking guidance and support from a pastor or a mentor, you can receive spiritual guidance and support, and you can grow in your relationship with God, and you can make your fast more meaningful and more purposeful, and you can receive blessings and grace.

CHAPTER TWO

INTRODUCTION TO BREAKFAST AND BRUNCH RECIPES FOR THE DANIEL FAST

Breakfast and brunch are important meals that provide the fuel and nutrients you need to start your day off right. During the Daniel Fast, it's important to choose breakfast and brunch foods that are both delicious and nutritious, and that will help you stay satisfied and energized throughout the day.

In this chapter, you'll find a variety of smoothie, oatmeal, granola, and breakfast bowl recipes that are suitable for the Daniel Fast and that will help you make the most of your breakfast and brunch meals. Each recipe includes a list of ingredients, step-by-step instructions, and nutritional information to help you plan and prepare your meals.

The Importance Of A Nutritious Breakfast

A nutritious breakfast is an important part of a healthy diet, and it can provide numerous benefits for your physical and mental health, as well as for your productivity and well-being.

Some of the benefits of a nutritious breakfast include:

1. Fueling your body and your brain: A nutritious breakfast can provide your body and your brain with the energy and the nutrients that they need to function optimally, and it can help you to avoid feelings of fatigue, irritability, and hunger throughout the day.

2. Improving your mood and your cognitive function: A nutritious breakfast can help to improve your mood and your cognitive function, and it can enhance your memory, your focus, and your concentration.

3. Promoting weight management: A nutritious breakfast can help to promote weight management, and it can reduce your risk of obesity, type 2 diabetes, and other health conditions.

4. Enhancing your physical performance: A nutritious breakfast can enhance your physical performance, and it can help you to feel stronger, more energetic,

and more capable of tackling your daily tasks and challenges.

5. Boosting your immune system: A nutritious breakfast can boost your immune system, and it can help you to stay healthy and to prevent illness and infections.

To ensure that you are getting a nutritious breakfast, you should aim to include a variety of whole, unprocessed, and minimally processed foods in your meals, such as whole grains, fruits, vegetables, lean proteins, and healthy fats. You should also avoid or limit sugary, high-fat, and unhealthy foods, and you should drink plenty of water, as it is essential for hydration and for the proper functioning of your body and your brain.

Tips For Making The Most Of Your Breakfast And Brunch Meals During The Daniel Fast

SMOOTHIE RECIPES

Smoothies are a great way to get a quick and easy breakfast or snack on the go. They are also a great way to incorporate a variety of fruits and vegetables into your diet. In this chapter, you'll find recipes for three delicious smoothies: a Tropical Smoothie, a Green Smoothie, and a Berry Smoothie.

Recipe 1: Tropical Smoothie

A tropical smoothie is a refreshing and nourishing drink that is made by blending together a variety of tropical fruits, such as pineapple, mango, banana, coconut, and papaya, along with other ingredients, such as yogurt, milk, ice, and honey. Tropical smoothies are a great way to enjoy the flavors and the nutrients of tropical fruits, and to hydrate and refresh your body, and they are easy to customize and to prepare, and they are suitable for a variety of dietary needs and preferences.

To make a tropical smoothie, you will need the following ingredients:

- 1 cup of pineapple chunks
- 1 cup of mango chunks
- 1 banana

- 1/2 cup of coconut milk
- 1/2 cup of plain yogurt
- 1 cup of ice
- 1 tablespoon of honey (optional)

To make a tropical smoothie, you will need to:

1. Wash and chop the pineapple and the mango into small chunks, and peel and slice the banana.
2. Place the pineapple, the mango, the banana, the coconut milk, the yogurt, and the ice in a blender.
3. Blend the ingredients together until smooth and creamy.
4. Add the honey (optional) and blend again until well combined.
5. Pour the tropical smoothie into a glass, and enjoy immediately.

You can serve the tropical smoothie as is, or you can garnish it with fresh fruit, coconut flakes, or a sprig of mint, and you can serve it chilled or over ice, depending on your preference. You can also customize the tropical smoothie by adding or substituting other ingredients, such as spinach, kale, chia seeds, or protein powder, and you can adjust the sweetness or the thickness to your liking.

I hope this information helps you to make a delicious and nourishing tropical smoothie, and that it helps you to enjoy the flavors and the nutrients of tropical fruits, and to hydrate and refresh your body. Remember, tropical smoothies are a great way to add variety and flavor to your diet, and to support your health and well-being, and they are fun and easy to prepare, and they are suitable for a variety of dietary needs and preferences. Enjoy!

Recipe 2: Green Smoothie

A green smoothie is a nutritious and refreshing drink that is made by blending together a variety of leafy green vegetables, such as spinach, kale, collard greens, or lettuce, along with other ingredients, such as fruit, yogurt, milk, ice, and honey. Green smoothies are a great way to incorporate more greens into your diet, and to boost your intake of vitamins, minerals, and antioxidants, and they are easy to customize and to prepare, and they are suitable for a variety of dietary needs and preferences.

To make a green smoothie, you will need the following ingredients:

- 2 cups of spinach or kale
- 1 banana
- 1 cup of fruit (such as berries, mango, or pineapple)
- 1 cup of unsweetened almond milk

- 1 cup of ice
- 1 tablespoon of honey (optional)

To make a green smoothie, you will need to:

1. Wash and chop the spinach or kale into small pieces, and peel and slice the banana.
2. Place the spinach or kale, the banana, the fruit, the almond milk, and the ice in a blender.
3. Blend the ingredients together until smooth and creamy.
4. Add the honey (optional) and blend again until well combined.
5. Pour the green smoothie into a glass, and enjoy immediately.

You can serve the green smoothie as is, or you can garnish it with fresh fruit, nuts, or seeds, and you can serve it chilled or over ice, depending on your preference. You can also customize the green smoothie by adding or substituting other ingredients, such as protein powder, chia seeds, or avocado, and you can adjust the sweetness or the thickness to your liking.

I hope this information helps you to make a delicious and nourishing green smoothie, and that it helps you to incorporate more greens into your diet, and to boost your intake of vitamins, minerals, and antioxidants.

Remember, green smoothies are a great way to support your health and well-being, and they are fun and easy to prepare, and they are suitable for a variety of dietary needs and preferences. Enjoy!

Recipe 3: Berry Smoothie

A berry smoothie is a tasty and nutritious drink that is made by blending together a variety of berries, such as strawberries, raspberries, blueberries, or blackberries, along with other ingredients, such as yogurt, milk, ice, and honey. Berry smoothies are a great way to enjoy the flavors and the nutrients of berries, and to support your health and well-being, and they are easy to customize and to prepare, and they are suitable for a variety of dietary needs and preferences.

To make a berry smoothie, you will need the following ingredients:

- 1 cup of mixed berries (such as strawberries, raspberries, blueberries, or blackberries)
- 1 banana
- 1 cup of unsweetened almond milk
- 1 cup of plain yogurt
- 1 cup of ice

- 1 tablespoon of honey (optional)

To make a berry smoothie, you will need to:

1. Wash and chop the berries, and peel and slice the banana.
2. Place the berries, the banana, the almond milk, the yogurt, and the ice in a blender.
3. Blend the ingredients together until smooth and creamy.
4. Add the honey (optional) and blend again until well combined.
5. Pour the berry smoothie into a glass, and enjoy immediately.

You can serve the berry smoothie as is, or you can garnish it with fresh berries, nuts, or seeds, and you can serve it chilled or over ice, depending on your preference. You can also customize the berry smoothie by adding or substituting other ingredients, such as protein powder, chia seeds, or avocado, and you can adjust the sweetness or the thickness to your liking.

I hope this information helps you to make a delicious and nourishing berry smoothie, and that it helps you to enjoy the flavors and the nutrients of berries, and to support your health and well-being. Remember, berry smoothies are a great way to add variety and flavor to your diet, and they are fun and easy to prepare, and they are suitable for a variety of dietary needs and preferences. Enjoy!

OATMEAL RECIPES

Oatmeal is another classic breakfast food that is easy to make and suitable for the Daniel Fast. In this chapter, you'll find recipes for three tasty oatmeal variations: Apple Cinnamon Oatmeal, Banana Nut Oatmeal, and Berry Oatmeal.

Recipe 1: Apple Cinnamon Oatmeal

Apple Cinnamon Oatmeal is a perfect plant-based nutrition that is made by cooking oats with apples, cinnamon, and other ingredients, such as milk, water, honey, and nuts. It is a warm and comforting breakfast dish. It is dairy-free and simple to make. It is also a perfect option for whenever you need something quick and satisfying. Full of fiber, protein and warm spices paired with a subtle sweetness from honey. This healthy oatmeal breakfast recipe is filling, as oats and pecans are high in protein and perfect for satisfying hunger cravings.

To make apple cinnamon oatmeal, you will need the following ingredients:

- 1 cup of old-fashioned oats
- 2 cups of water
- 1 cup of unsweetened almond milk
- 1 medium apple, peeled, cored, and diced
- 1 teaspoon of cinnamon
- 1 tablespoon of honey (optional)
- 1/4 cup of chopped nuts (such as almonds, walnuts, or pecans)

To make apple cinnamon oatmeal, you will need to:

1. Place the oats, the water, and the almond milk in a medium saucepan, and bring to a boil over high heat.
2. Reduce the heat to medium-low, and add the apple and the cinnamon.
3. Simmer the oats until they are tender and the liquid is absorbed, stirring occasionally, about 10-15 minutes.
4. Remove the saucepan from the heat, and stir in the honey (optional).
5. Serve the oatmeal in bowls, and top with the chopped nuts.

You can serve the apple cinnamon oatmeal as is, or you can garnish it with additional fruit, nuts, or seeds, and you can serve it hot or warm, depending on your preference. You can also customize the apple cinnamon oatmeal by adding or substituting other ingredients, such as raisins, coconut flakes, or protein powder, and you can adjust the sweetness or the thickness to your liking. Feel free to use maple syrup in place of honey for a vegan option. You can use any type of apple for this recipe. We can recommend Granny Smith, Gala, Honey crisp, etc. And, for even creamer options, stir in your choice of milk. Don't like apples? Swap it with spume pairs or peaches.

Recipe 2: Banana Nut Oatmeal

Banana nut oatmeal is a delectable and nutritious breakfast dish made by cooking oats with bananas, nuts, and different fixings, like milk, water, honey, and cinnamon. Banana nut oats is a delectable and feeding method for beginning your day, and it is wealthy in fiber, protein, and supplements, it is not challenging to redo and get ready, and they are reasonable for various dietary requirements and inclinations.

To make banana nut oatmeal, you will need the following ingredients:

- 1 cup of old-fashioned oats
- 2 cups of water
- 1 cup of unsweetened almond milk
- 2 medium bananas, peeled and mashed
- 1/2 cup of chopped nuts (such as almonds, walnuts, or pecans)
- 1 teaspoon of cinnamon
- 1 tablespoon of honey (optional)

To make banana nut oatmeal, you will need to:

1. Place the oats, the water, and the almond milk in a medium saucepan, and bring to a boil over high heat.
2. Reduce the heat to medium-low, and add the mashed bananas and the cinnamon.
3. Simmer the oats until they are tender and the liquid is absorbed, stirring occasionally, about 10-15 minutes.
4. Remove the saucepan from the heat, and stir in the honey (optional).
5. Serve the oatmeal in bowls, and top with the chopped nuts.

You can serve the banana nut oatmeal as is, or you can garnish it with additional fruit, nuts, or seeds, and you can serve it hot or warm, depending on your preference. You can also customize the banana nut oatmeal by adding or substituting other ingredients, such as raisins, coconut flakes, or protein powder, and you can adjust the sweetness or the thickness to your liking.

Recipe 3: Berry Oatmeal

Berry oatmeal is a flavorful and nutritious breakfast dish that is made by cooking oats with berries, and other ingredients, such as milk, water, honey, and nuts. Berry oatmeal is a delicious and nourishing way to start your day, and it is rich in fiber, protein, and nutrients, and it is easy to customize and to prepare, and it is suitable for a variety of dietary needs and preferences.

To make berry oatmeal, you will need the following ingredients:

- 1 cup of old-fashioned oats
- 2 cups of water
- 1 cup of unsweetened almond milk
- 1 cup of mixed berries (such as strawberries, raspberries, blueberries, or blackberries)

- 1/2 cup of chopped nuts (such as almonds, walnuts, or pecans)
- 1 tablespoon of honey (optional)

To make berry oatmeal, you will need to:

1. Place the oats, the water, and the almond milk in a medium saucepan, and bring to a boil over high heat.
2. Reduce the heat to medium-low, and add the mixed berries.
3. Simmer the oats until they are tender and the liquid is absorbed, stirring occasionally, about 10-15 minutes.
4. Remove the saucepan from the heat, and stir in the honey (optional).
5. Serve the oatmeal in bowls, and top with the chopped nuts.

You can serve the berry oatmeal as is, or you can garnish it with additional fruit, nuts, or seeds, and you can serve it hot or warm, depending on your preference. You can also customize the berry oatmeal by adding or substituting other ingredients, such as raisins, coconut flakes, or protein powder, and you can adjust the sweetness or the thickness to your liking.

GRANOLA RECIPES

Granola is a tasty and crunchy breakfast or snack that is perfect for topping your oatmeal, yogurt, or smoothie bowls. In this chapter, you'll find recipes for three delicious granola variations: Maple Granola, Peanut Butter Granola, and Coconut Granola.

Recipe 1: Maple Granola

Maple granola is a crunchy and delicious breakfast or snack food that is made by baking oats, nuts, and seeds with maple syrup, oil, and other ingredients, such as cinnamon, vanilla, and dried fruit. Maple granola is a tasty and nourishing way to enjoy a variety of flavors and textures, and it is rich in fiber, protein, and nutrients, and it is easy to customize and to prepare, and it is suitable for a variety of dietary needs and preferences.

To make maple granola, you will need the following ingredients:

- 4 cups of old-fashioned oats
- 1 cup of chopped nuts (such as almonds, walnuts, or pecans)
- 1/2 cup of sunflower seeds or pumpkin seeds
- 1/2 cup of maple syrup
- 1/4 cup of vegetable oil

- 1 teaspoon of cinnamon
- 1 teaspoon of vanilla extract
- 1 cup of dried fruit (such as raisins, cranberries, or apricots)

To make maple granola, you will need to:

1. Preheat the oven to 350°F (180°C). Line a large baking sheet with parchment paper.
2. In a large mixing bowl, combine the oats, the nuts, the seeds, the maple syrup, the oil, the cinnamon, and the vanilla extract, and stir well to combine.
3. Spread the mixture evenly on the prepared baking sheet.
4. Bake the granola for 15-20 minutes, or until it is golden brown and crunchy, stirring occasionally.
5. Remove the granola from the oven, and let it cool completely on the baking sheet.
6. Break the granola into small pieces, and stir in the dried fruit.
7. Store the granola in an airtight container at room temperature for up to 2 weeks.

You can serve the maple granola as is, or you can garnish it with additional nuts, seeds, or fruit, and you can serve it with milk, yogurt, or fruit, depending on your preference. You can also customize the maple granola by adding or substituting other ingredients, such as chocolate chips, coconut flakes, or protein powder, and you can adjust the sweetness or the crunchiness to your liking.

Recipe 2: Peanut Butter Granola

Peanut butter granola is a tasty and nutritious breakfast or snack food that is made by baking oats, nuts, and seeds with peanut butter, oil, and other ingredients, such as honey, cinnamon, and dried fruit. Peanut butter granola is a delicious and nourishing way to enjoy the flavors of peanut butter, and it is rich in fiber, protein, and nutrients, and it is easy to customize and to prepare, and it is suitable for a variety of dietary needs and preferences.

To make peanut butter granola, you will need the following ingredients:

- 4 cups of old-fashioned oats
- 1 cup of chopped nuts (such as almonds, walnuts, or pecans)
- 1/2 cup of sunflower seeds or pumpkin seeds
- 1/2 cup of peanut butter
- 1/4 cup of honey
- 1/4 cup of vegetable oil
- 1 teaspoon of cinnamon
- 1 teaspoon of vanilla extract

- 1 cup of dried fruit (such as raisins, cranberries, or apricots)

To make peanut butter granola, you will need to:

1. Preheat the oven to 350°F (180°C). Line a large baking sheet with parchment paper.
2. In a large mixing bowl, combine the oats, the nuts, the seeds, the peanut butter, the honey, the oil, the cinnamon, and the vanilla extract, and stir well to combine.
3. Spread the mixture evenly on the prepared baking sheet.
4. Bake the granola for 15-20 minutes, or until it is golden brown and crunchy, stirring occasionally.
5. Remove the granola from the oven, and let it cool completely on the baking sheet.
6. Break the granola into small pieces, and stir in the dried fruit.
7. Store the granola in an airtight container at room temperature for up to 2 weeks.

You can serve the peanut butter granola as is, or you can garnish it with additional nuts, seeds, or fruit, and you can serve it with milk, yogurt, or fruit, depending on your preference. You can also customize the peanut butter granola by adding or substituting other ingredients, such as chocolate chips, coconut flakes, or protein powder, and you can adjust the sweetness or the crunchiness to your liking.

Recipe 3: Coconut Granola

Coconut granola is a tropical and delicious breakfast or snack food that is made by baking oats, nuts, and seeds with coconut milk, oil, and other ingredients, such as honey, cinnamon, and dried fruit. Coconut granola is a tasty and nourishing way to enjoy the flavors of coconut, and it is rich in fiber, protein, and nutrients, and it is easy to customize and to prepare, and it is suitable for a variety of dietary needs and preferences.

To make coconut granola, you will need the following ingredients:

- 4 cups of old-fashioned oats
- 1 cup of chopped nuts (such as almonds, walnuts, or pecans)
- 1/2 cup of sunflower seeds or pumpkin seeds
- 1/2 cup of coconut milk
- 1/4 cup of honey
- 1/4 cup of vegetable oil
- 1 teaspoon of cinnamon
- 1 teaspoon of vanilla extract

- 1 cup of dried fruit (such as raisins, cranberries, or apricots)

To make coconut granola, you will need to:

1. Preheat the oven to 350°F (180°C). Line a large baking sheet with parchment paper.
2. In a large mixing bowl, combine the oats, the nuts, the seeds, the coconut milk, the honey, the oil, the cinnamon, and the vanilla extract, and stir well to combine.
3. Spread the mixture evenly on the prepared baking sheet.
4. Bake the granola for 15-20 minutes, or until it is golden brown and crunchy, stirring occasionally.
5. Remove the granola from the oven, and let it cool completely on the baking sheet.
6. Break the granola into small pieces, and stir in the dried fruit.
7. Store the granola in an airtight container at room temperature for up to 2 weeks.

You can serve the coconut granola as is, or you can garnish it with additional nuts, seeds, or fruit, and you can serve it with milk, yogurt, or fruit, depending on your preference. You can also customize the coconut granola by adding or substituting other ingredients, such as chocolate chips, coconut flakes, or protein powder, and you can adjust the sweetness or the crunchiness to your liking.

BREAKFAST BOWL RECIPES

Breakfast bowls are another popular breakfast option that allows you to combine a variety of ingredients in one convenient and tasty meal. In this chapter, you'll find recipes for three delicious breakfast bowls: an Acai Bowl, a Smoothie Bowl, and Overnight Oats.

Recipe 1: Acai Bowl

An acai bowl is a delicious and nutritious breakfast or snack food that is made by blending frozen acai berries with other ingredients, such as milk, fruit, and nuts, and then topping it with additional fruit, nuts, seeds, and other toppings. Acai bowls are a tasty and nourishing way to enjoy the flavors and nutrients of acai berries, and they are rich in fiber, protein, and antioxidants, and they are easy to customize and to prepare, and they are suitable for a variety of dietary needs and preferences.

To make an acai bowl, you will need the following ingredients:

- 1 packet of frozen acai berries

- 1 cup of milk or plant-based milk
- 1 banana
- 1 cup of frozen fruit (such as strawberries, mango, or pineapple)

To make an acai bowl, you will need to:

1. Place the acai berries, the milk, the banana, and the frozen fruit in a blender, and blend until smooth.
2. Pour the acai mixture into a bowl, and top with your favorite toppings, such as fruit, nuts, seeds, or granola.
3. Serve the acai bowl immediately, or freeze it for later.

You can customize the acai bowl by adding or substituting other ingredients, such as yogurt, honey, or protein powder, and you can adjust the sweetness or the thickness to your liking. Some popular toppings for acai bowls include sliced banana, strawberries, blueberries, raspberries, mango, pineapple, kiwi, coconut flakes, chia seeds, hemp seeds, and granola.

Recipe 2: Smoothie Bowl

A smoothie bowl is a delicious and nutritious breakfast or snack food that is made by blending fruit, vegetables, and other ingredients, such as milk, yogurt, and protein powder, and then topping it with additional fruit, nuts, seeds, and other toppings. Smoothie bowls are a tasty and nourishing way to enjoy a variety of flavors and textures, and they are rich in fiber, protein, and nutrients, and they are easy to customize and to prepare, and they are suitable for a variety of dietary needs and preferences.

To make a smoothie bowl, you will need the following ingredients:

- 1 cup of milk or plant-based milk
- 1 cup of yogurt or plant-based yogurt
- 1 banana
- 1 cup of frozen fruit (such as strawberries, mango, or pineapple)
- 1 cup of fresh or frozen vegetables (such as spinach, kale, or berries)

To make a smoothie bowl, you will need to:

1. Place the milk, the yogurt, the banana, the frozen fruit, and the vegetables in a blender, and blend until smooth.
2. Pour the smoothie mixture into a bowl, and top with your favorite toppings, such as fruit, nuts, seeds, or granola.
3. Serve the smoothie bowl immediately, or freeze it for later.

You can customize the smoothie bowl by adding or substituting other ingredients, such as honey, protein powder, or nuts, and you can adjust the sweetness or the thickness to your liking. Some popular toppings for smoothie bowls include sliced banana, strawberries, blueberries, raspberries, mango, pineapple, kiwi, coconut flakes, chia seeds, hemp seeds, and granola.

Recipe 3: Overnight Oats

Overnight oats are a delicious and nutritious breakfast or snack food that is made by soaking oats, milk, and other ingredients in a jar or a bowl overnight, and then topping it with additional ingredients in the morning. Overnight oats are a tasty and nourishing way to enjoy the flavors and textures of oats, and they are rich in fiber, protein, and nutrients, and they are easy to customize and to prepare, and they are suitable for a variety of dietary needs and preferences.

To make overnight oats, you will need the following ingredients:

- 1 cup of old-fashioned oats
- 1 cup of milk or plant-based milk
- 1 tablespoon of chia seeds
- 1 tablespoon of honey or maple syrup

- 1 teaspoon of vanilla extract

To make overnight oats, you will need to:

1. In a jar or a bowl, combine the oats, the milk, the chia seeds, the honey, and the vanilla extract, and stir well to combine.
2. Cover the jar or the bowl with a lid or plastic wrap, and refrigerate it overnight, or for at least 4 hours.
3. In the morning, stir the oats, and top them with your favorite toppings, such as fruit, nuts, seeds, or yogurt.
4. Serve the overnight oats immediately, or refrigerate them for later.

You can customize the overnight oats by adding or substituting other ingredients, such as yogurt, fruit, protein powder, or nuts, and you can adjust the sweetness or the thickness to your liking. Some popular toppings for overnight oats include sliced banana, strawberries, blueberries, raspberries, mango, pineapple, kiwi, coconut flakes, chia seeds, hemp seeds, and granola.

CHAPTER THREE

[Soups and Salads: Recipes for hearty soups, light salads, and other nourishing dishes that are perfect for lunch or dinner.]

INTRODUCTION TO SOUP AND SALAD RECIPES FOR THE DANIEL FAST

Soups and salads are an important part of a healthy and balanced diet, and they can be especially useful during the Daniel Fast. Soups are a great way to get a variety of nutrients in one convenient and satisfying meal, and they are easy to make and store for future meals. Salads are a refreshing and nourishing way to incorporate a variety of fruits and vegetables into your diet.

In this chapter, you'll find a variety of soup and salad recipes that are suitable for the Daniel Fast and that will help you make the most of your soup and salad meals. Each recipe includes a list of ingredients, step-by-step instructions, and nutritional information to help you plan and prepare your meals.

The Importance Of Incorporating Soups And Salads Into Your Diet

Soups and salads are nutritious and versatile dishes that can be a valuable addition to your diet, and they can provide numerous benefits for your physical and mental health.

Some of the benefits of incorporating soups and salads into your diet include:

1. Increasing your intake of fruits and vegetables: Soups and salads are an excellent way to increase your intake of fruits and vegetables, which are rich in fiber, vitamins, minerals, and antioxidants, and which can help to protect against chronic diseases, such as heart disease, cancer, and diabetes.

2. Promoting weight management: Soups and salads are generally low in calories, fat, and sugar, and they can help to fill you up, and to reduce your risk of overeating and weight gain.

3. Improving digestion: Soups and salads can help to improve digestion, and they can provide your body with the hydration and the fiber that it needs to

eliminate waste and toxins, and to support the health of your gut micro biome.

4. Boosting your immune system: Soups and salads can boost your immune system, and they can help you to stay healthy and to prevent illness and infections, and they can also help to reduce inflammation and to support the health of your skin, your hair, and your nails.

5. Enhancing your mood and your cognitive function: Soups and salads can help to improve your mood and your cognitive function, and they can enhance your energy, your focus, and your concentration, and they can also help to reduce stress, anxiety, and depression.

To incorporate soups and salads into your diet, you can try a variety of recipes, and you can use different ingredients, such as leafy greens, vegetables, beans, grains, nuts, seeds, and herbs, and you can customize them to your taste and dietary needs, and you can use dressings, sauces, and spices to add flavor and depth to your dishes. You can also prepare soups and salads in advance, and you can freeze or refrigerate them for later, and you can enjoy them as a main course, a side dish, or a snack.

Tips For Making The Most Of Your Soup And Salad Meals During The Daniel Fast

SOUP RECIPES

Recipe 1: Tomato Soup

This classic soup is made with ripe tomatoes, onions, and garlic, and it's seasoned with a blend of herbs and spices. It's a comforting and satisfying meal that is perfect for cold weather.

Here is a simple and flavorful recipe for tomato soup that you can enjoy during the Daniel Fast, or any other time:

Ingredients:

- 1 tablespoon olive oil
- 1 onion, diced
- 2 cloves garlic, minced
- 1 can diced tomatoes
- 1 quart vegetable broth
- 1 teaspoon dried basil

- 1 teaspoon dried oregano
- Salt and pepper to taste

Instructions:

1. Heat the olive oil in a large pot over medium heat.
2. Add the onion and the garlic, and cook until the onion is translucent, about 5 minutes.
3. Add the diced tomatoes, the vegetable broth, the basil, the oregano, and the salt and pepper, and bring to a boil.
4. Reduce the heat to low, and simmer for 20 minutes, or until the soup is hot and flavorful.
5. Serve hot, garnished with fresh herbs, if desired.

You can also add other vegetables, such as bell peppers, carrots, or zucchini, to the soup, and you can use fresh or canned tomatoes, depending on your preference and availability. You can also use different herbs and spices, such as thyme, marjoram, or cumin, to add depth and complexity to the flavor of the soup. You can also blend the soup in a blender or with an immersion blender, for a smooth and creamy texture.

Recipe 2: Black Bean Soup

This hearty and flavorful soup is made with black beans, vegetables, and a variety of spices. It's a protein-packed meal that is sure to fill you up.

Here is a simple and delicious recipe for black bean soup that you can enjoy during the Daniel Fast, or any other time:

Ingredients:

- 1 tablespoon olive oil
- 1 onion, diced
- 2 cloves garlic, minced
- 1 red bell pepper, diced
- 1 can diced tomatoes
- 1 can black beans, drained and rinsed
- 1 quart vegetable broth
- 1 teaspoon chili powder
- 1 teaspoon cumin
- 1 teaspoon paprika
- Salt and pepper to taste

Instructions:

1. Heat the olive oil in a large pot over medium heat.

2. Add the onion and the garlic, and cook until the onion is translucent, about 5 minutes.
3. Add the bell pepper and the diced tomatoes, and cook for an additional 5 minutes.
4. Add the black beans, the vegetable broth, the chili powder, the cumin, the paprika, and the salt and pepper, and bring to a boil.
5. Reduce the heat to low, and simmer for 20 minutes, or until the vegetables are tender.
6. Serve hot, garnished with fresh herbs, if desired.

You can also add other vegetables, such as carrots, celery, or sweet potato, to the soup, and you can use fresh or canned tomatoes, depending on your preference and availability. You can also use different herbs and spices, such as basil, oregano, or thyme, to add depth and complexity to the flavor of the soup. You can also blend the soup in a blender or with an immersion blender, for a smooth and creamy texture.

Recipe 3: Butternut Squash Soup

This creamy and velvety soup is made with roasted butternut squash, onions, and spices. It's a delicious and nourishing meal that is perfect for fall.

Here is a simple and flavorful recipe for butternut squash soup that you can enjoy during the Daniel Fast, or any other time:

Ingredients:

- 1 tablespoon olive oil
- 1 onion, diced
- 2 cloves garlic, minced
- 1 butternut squash, peeled, seeded, and diced
- 1 quart vegetable broth
- 1 teaspoon dried thyme
- 1 teaspoon dried marjoram
- Salt and pepper to taste

Instructions:

1. Heat the olive oil in a large pot over medium heat.
2. Add the onion and the garlic, and cook until the onion is translucent, about 5 minutes.
3. Add the butternut squash and the vegetable broth, and bring to a boil.
4. Reduce the heat to low, and simmer for 30 minutes, or until the squash is tender.
5. Add the thyme, the marjoram, and the salt and pepper, and stir well.
6. Using a blender or an immersion blender, blend the soup until smooth and creamy.

7. Serve hot, garnished with fresh herbs, if desired.

You can also add other vegetables, such as carrots, sweet potatoes, or parsnips, to the soup, and you can use different herbs and spices, such as basil, oregano, or cumin, to add depth and complexity to the flavor of the soup. You can also serve the soup with a dollop of coconut cream, or a sprinkle of toasted nuts or seeds, for a decadent and satisfying touch.

SALAD RECIPES

Recipe 1: Caesar Salad

A **Caesar salad** is a green tossed salad of romaine lettuce and croutons dressed with lemon juice (or lime juice), olive oil, egg, Worcestershire sauce, anchovies, garlic, Dijon mustard, Parmesan cheese, and black pepper. Caesar salads are so satisfying because they are perfectly balanced in the macronutrients you need. You have the right amount of protein with the eggs, healthy fats with the parmesan cheese and dressing, and carbohydrates for energy to feel satisfied.

Common ingredients in many recipes include:

- romaine or cos lettuce
- olive oil
- crushed garlic
- salt
- Dijon mustard
- black pepper
- lemon juice
- Worcestershire sauce
- anchovies
- raw or coddled eggs
- grated Parmesan cheese
- croutons

Variations include varying the leaf, adding meat such as grilled chicken or bacon, or omitting ingredients such as anchovies and eggs.

Vegan versions may substitute capers for anchovies, and replace eggs with tahini.

Here is a simple and delicious recipe for Caesar salad that you can enjoy during the Daniel Fast, or any other time:

Ingredients:

- 1 head romaine lettuce, washed and chopped
- 1 cup cherry tomatoes, halved
- 1 cup croutons (optional)
- 1 cup grated Parmesan cheese

For the dressing:

- 1/2 cup mayonnaise
- 1/4 cup sour cream
- 2 tablespoons lemon juice
- 1 clove garlic, minced
- 1 teaspoon Dijon mustard
- 1 teaspoon Worcestershire sauce
- Salt and pepper to taste

Instructions:

1. In a large bowl, combine the romaine lettuce, the cherry tomatoes, the croutons (if using), and the Parmesan cheese.
2. In a small bowl, whisk together the mayonnaise, the sour cream, the lemon juice, the garlic, the mustard, the Worcestershire sauce, and the salt and pepper.
3. Pour the dressing over the salad, and toss well to coat.
4. Serve immediately, garnished with additional Parmesan cheese, if desired.

You can also add other ingredients to the salad, such as grilled chicken, boiled eggs, bacon, or avocado, to make it more filling and satisfying. You can also use different types of lettuce, such as iceberg, arugula, or spinach, depending on your preference and availability. You can also use different herbs and spices, such as basil, oregano, or cumin, to add depth and complexity to the flavor of the salad.

Recipe 2: Kale Salad

This nutrient-rich salad is made with hearty kale, crunchy nuts, and a variety of fruits and vegetables. It's a refreshing and satisfying meal that is perfect for any time of day.

Here is a simple and nutritious recipe for kale salad that you can enjoy during the Daniel Fast, or any other time:

Ingredients:

- 1 bunch kale, washed and chopped
- 1 cup cherry tomatoes, halved
- 1 cup croutons (optional)
- 1 cup grated Parmesan cheese

For the dressing:

- 1/2 cup olive oil
- 1/4 cup lemon juice
- 1 clove garlic, minced
- 1 teaspoon Dijon mustard
- 1 teaspoon honey
- Salt and pepper to taste

Instructions:

1. In a large bowl, combine the kale, the cherry tomatoes, the croutons (if using), and the Parmesan cheese.
2. In a small bowl, whisk together the olive oil, the lemon juice, the garlic, the mustard, the honey, and the salt and pepper.
3. Pour the dressing over the salad, and toss well to coat.
4. Serve immediately, garnished with additional Parmesan cheese, if desired.

You can also add other ingredients to the salad, such as grilled chicken, boiled eggs, bacon, or avocado, to make it more filling and satisfying. You can also use different types of lettuce, such as romaine, arugula, or spinach, depending on your preference and availability. You can also use different herbs and spices, such as basil, oregano, or cumin, to add depth and complexity to the flavor of the salad.

Recipe 3: Quinoa Salad

This protein-packed salad is made with fluffy quinoa, a variety of vegetables, and a flavorful dressing. It's a satisfying and nourishing meal that is perfect for lunch or dinner.

Here is a simple and flavorful recipe for quinoa salad that you can enjoy during the Daniel Fast, or any other time:

Ingredients:

- 1 cup quinoa, rinsed and drained
- 2 cups water
- 1 cup cherry tomatoes, halved
- 1 cup cucumber, diced
- 1 cup bell peppers, diced
- 1 cup red onions, diced
- 1 cup feta cheese, crumbled

For the dressing:

- 1/2 cup olive oil
- 1/4 cup red wine vinegar
- 1 clove garlic, minced
- 1 teaspoon Dijon mustard
- 1 teaspoon honey
- Salt and pepper to taste

Instructions:

1. In a medium pot, bring the quinoa and the water to a boil. Reduce the heat to low, and simmer for 15 minutes, or until the quinoa is tender and the water is absorbed.

2. Transfer the quinoa to a large bowl, and let it cool to room temperature.
3. Add the cherry tomatoes, the cucumber, the bell peppers, the red onions, and the feta cheese to the quinoa, and toss well to combine.
4. In a small bowl, whisk together the olive oil, the red wine vinegar, the garlic, the mustard, the honey, and the salt and pepper.
5. Pour the dressing over the salad, and toss well to coat.
6. Serve immediately, garnished with additional feta cheese, if desired.

You can also add other ingredients to the salad, such as grilled chicken, boiled eggs, bacon, or avocado, to make it more filling and satisfying. You can also use different types of lettuce, such as romaine, arugula, or spinach, depending on your preference and availability. You can also use different herbs and spices, such as basil, oregano, or cumin, to add depth and complexity to the flavor of the salad.

CHAPTER FOUR

[Main Courses: Recipes for plant-based proteins, grains, and
vegetables that is sure to satisfy your hunger and your taste buds.]

INTRODUCTION TO MAIN DISH
RECIPES FOR THE DANIEL FAST

As you embark on the Daniel Fast, it's important to
choose main dishes that are both delicious and nutritious,
and that will help you stay satisfied and energized
throughout the day. In this chapter, you'll find a variety of
main dish recipes that are suitable for the Daniel Fast and
that will help you make the most of your meals. Each
recipe includes a list of ingredients, step-by-step
instructions, and nutritional information to help you plan
and prepare your meals.

Ideas For Serving Main Dishes As Part Of A Balanced And Satisfying Meal

Here are some ideas for serving main dishes as part of a
balanced and satisfying meal:

1. Include a variety of vegetables: Aim to include a variety of colorful vegetables in your meals, as they provide a range of essential nutrients and can help you feel fuller and more satisfied. You can serve your main dish with a side of steamed or roasted vegetables, a salad, or a soup.

2. Add a source of protein: A source of protein can help you feel full and satisfied, and it can help to repair and build muscle tissue. Some good plant-based protein options for the Daniel Fast include beans, lentils, tofu, and tempeh. You can serve your main dish with a side of beans, lentils, or tofu, or you can incorporate them into your dish as an ingredient.

3. Choose whole grains: Whole grains are an excellent source of fiber, which can help to keep you feeling full and satisfied. Some good options for the Daniel Fast include quinoa, brown rice, and whole grain pasta. You can serve your main dish with a side of whole grains, or you can incorporate them into your dish as an ingredient.

4. Add healthy fats: Healthy fats, such as olive oil, avocado, and nuts, can help to improve the absorption of certain nutrients and can help to keep you feeling full and satisfied. You can drizzle your main dish with a little bit of olive oil, add

some sliced avocado on top, or sprinkle some nuts or seeds over your dish.

5. Include a source of hydration: It's important to stay hydrated throughout the day, and you can do this by including a source of hydration in your meals. Some good options for the Daniel Fast include water, herbal tea, and broth-based soups. You can serve your main dish with a glass of water or a cup of herbal tea, or you can incorporate broth-based soups into your meal.

6. Serve smaller portions: It's important to listen to your body's hunger and fullness cues, and this can be easier to do when you serve yourself smaller portions. You can start by filling half of your plate with vegetables, a quarter with a source of protein, and a quarter with a source of whole grains. You can then adjust the proportions based on your appetite and hunger levels.

7. Make it visually appealing: The appearance of your meal can have an impact on your enjoyment of it, so take a few extra minutes to make your dish look visually appealing. You can do this by arranging your ingredients in an attractive way on the plate, using colorful vegetables, and garnishing your dish with herbs or nuts.

8. Take your time: It takes about 20 minutes for your brain to register that you are full, so take your time when you are eating and savor each bite. Avoid distractions such as screens or multitasking while you are eating, and focus on the taste, texture, and appearance of your food.

9. Practice mindful eating: Mindful eating involves paying attention to your body's hunger and fullness cues, as well as the sights, sounds, and smells of your food. This can help you to enjoy your meals more and to feel more satisfied after you eat. You can practice mindful eating by focusing on your food, taking small bites, and chewing slowly.

10. Plan ahead: Planning your meals in advance can help you to make healthier choices and to feel more organized and in control. You can plan your meals for the week by making a grocery list, prepping your ingredients in advance, and packing your meals for the day. This can help you to save time and effort, and it can also help you to stay on track with your healthy eating goals.

Tips For Choosing And Preparing Main Dishes That Are Suitable For The Daniel Fast

GRILLED VEGETABLE RECIPES

Recipe 1: Grilled Eggplant

This delicious and savory recipe is made with slices of eggplant that are grilled to perfection and topped with a flavorful marinade.

Here is a simple and flavorful recipe for grilled eggplant that you can enjoy during the Daniel Fast, or any other time:

Ingredients:

- 1 eggplant, sliced into 1/2-inch rounds
- 1 tablespoon olive oil
- 1 teaspoon dried oregano
- 1 teaspoon dried basil
- 1 teaspoon dried thyme

- Salt and pepper to taste

Instructions:

1. Preheat the grill to medium heat.
2. In a small bowl, combine the olive oil, the oregano, the basil, the thyme, and the salt and pepper.
3. Brush the eggplant slices with the oil mixture, on both sides.
4. Place the eggplant slices on the grill, and cook for 5-7 minutes on each side, or until they are tender and have grill marks.
5. Serve the eggplant hot, garnished with fresh herbs, if desired.

You can also add other vegetables to the grill, such as bell peppers, onions, or zucchini, and you can use different herbs and spices, such as cumin, paprika, or garlic, to add depth and complexity to the flavor of the vegetables. You can also serve the grilled vegetables with a dipping sauce, such as tzatziki, hummus, or ranch dressing, for a more satisfying and flavorful experience.

Recipe 2: Grilled Portobello Mushrooms

These meaty and flavorful mushrooms are a great plant-based option for the main dish of your meal.

Here is a simple and flavorful recipe for grilled Portobello mushrooms that you can enjoy during the Daniel Fast, or any other time:

Ingredients:

- 4 Portobello mushrooms, stems removed
- 1 tablespoon olive oil
- 1 teaspoon dried oregano
- 1 teaspoon dried basil
- 1 teaspoon dried thyme
- Salt and pepper to taste

Instructions:

1. Preheat the grill to medium heat.
2. In a small bowl, combine the olive oil, the oregano, the basil, the thyme, and the salt and pepper.
3. Brush the Portobello mushrooms with the oil mixture, on both sides.
4. Place the mushrooms on the grill, and cook for 5-7 minutes on each side, or until they are tender and have grill marks.
5. Serve the mushrooms hot, garnished with fresh herbs, if desired.

You can also add other vegetables to the grill, such as bell peppers, onions, or zucchini, and you can use different herbs and spices, such as cumin, paprika, or garlic, to add depth and complexity to the flavor of the vegetables. You can also serve the grilled mushrooms with a dipping sauce, such as tzatziki, hummus, or ranch dressing, for a more satisfying and flavorful experience.

Recipe 3: Grilled Zucchini

This simple and satisfying recipe is made with slices of zucchini that are grilled to perfection and topped with a flavorful marinade.

Here is a simple and flavorful recipe for grilled zucchini that you can enjoy during the Daniel Fast, or any other time:

Ingredients:

- 2 zucchini, sliced into 1/2-inch rounds
- 1 tablespoon olive oil
- 1 teaspoon dried oregano
- 1 teaspoon dried basil
- 1 teaspoon dried thyme
- Salt and pepper to taste

Instructions:

1. Preheat the grill to medium heat.

2. In a small bowl, combine the olive oil, the oregano, the basil, the thyme, and the salt and pepper.
3. Brush the zucchini slices with the oil mixture, on both sides.
4. Place the zucchini slices on the grill, and cook for 5-7 minutes on each side, or until they are tender and have grill marks.
5. Serve the zucchini hot, garnished with fresh herbs, if desired.

You can also add other vegetables to the grill, such as bell peppers, onions, or eggplant, and you can use different herbs and spices, such as cumin, paprika, or garlic, to add depth and complexity to the flavor of the vegetables. You can also serve the grilled zucchini with a dipping sauce, such as tzatziki, hummus, or ranch dressing, for a more satisfying and flavorful experience.

STIR-FRY RECIPES

Recipe 1: Tofu Stir-Fry

This flavorful and satisfying stir-fry is made with tofu, vegetables, and a savory sauce.

Here is a simple and flavorful recipe for tofu stir-fry that you can enjoy during the Daniel Fast, or any other time:

Ingredients:

- 1 block firm tofu, drained and cubed
- 1 tablespoon olive oil
- 1 cup bell peppers, diced
- 1 cup onions, diced
- 1 cup carrots, sliced
- 1 cup broccoli florets
- 1 cup cherry tomatoes, halved
- 1 cup mushrooms, sliced
- 1 cup snow peas

For the sauce:

- 1/2 cup vegetable broth
- 1/4 cup soy sauce
- 1 tablespoon cornstarch
- 1 teaspoon sesame oil
- 1 teaspoon honey
- 1 clove garlic, minced
- 1 teaspoon ginger, minced
- 1 teaspoon chili flakes (optional)

Instructions:

1. In a small bowl, whisk together the vegetable broth, the soy sauce, the cornstarch, the sesame oil, the honey, the garlic, the ginger, and the chili flakes (if using). Set aside.
2. Heat the olive oil in a large wok or skillet over medium-high heat.
3. Add the tofu, and cook for 5 minutes, stirring occasionally, until it is browned and crispy.
4. Add the bell peppers, the onions, the carrots, the broccoli, the cherry tomatoes, the mushrooms, and the snow peas to the wok, and cook for 5 minutes, stirring occasionally, until they are tender and lightly caramelized.
5. Pour the sauce over the vegetables and tofu, and cook for 2-3 minutes, stirring constantly, until the sauce thickens and coats the vegetables and tofu.
6. Serve the stir-fry hot, garnished with fresh herbs, if desired.

You can also add other ingredients to the stir-fry, such as grilled chicken, beef, or shrimp, or other types of vegetables, such as zucchini, eggplant, or bok choy, depending on your preference and availability. You can also use different sauces, such as peanut sauce, hoisin sauce, or coconut curry sauce, to add depth and complexity to the flavor of the stir-fry. You can also serve the stir-fry with a side of rice, quinoa, or noodles, to make it more filling and satisfying.

Recipe 2: Vegetable Stir-Fry

This colorful and nourishing stir-fry is made with a variety of vegetables, such as bell peppers, onions, carrots, and broccoli, and a savory sauce.

Here is a simple and flavorful recipe for vegetable stir-fry that you can enjoy during the Daniel Fast, or any other time:

Ingredients:

- 1 tablespoon olive oil
- 1 cup bell peppers, diced
- 1 cup onions, diced
- 1 cup carrots, sliced
- 1 cup broccoli florets
- 1 cup cherry tomatoes, halved
- 1 cup mushrooms, sliced
- 1 cup snow peas

For the sauce:

- 1/2 cup vegetable broth

- 1/4 cup soy sauce
- 1 tablespoon cornstarch
- 1 teaspoon sesame oil
- 1 teaspoon honey
- 1 clove garlic, minced
- 1 teaspoon ginger, minced
- 1 teaspoon chili flakes (optional)

Instructions:

1. In a small bowl, whisk together the vegetable broth, the soy sauce, the cornstarch, the sesame oil, the honey, the garlic, the ginger, and the chili flakes (if using). Set aside.
2. Heat the olive oil in a large wok or skillet over medium-high heat.
3. Add the bell peppers, the onions, the carrots, the broccoli, the cherry tomatoes, the mushrooms, and the snow peas to the wok, and cook for 5 minutes, stirring occasionally, until they are tender and lightly caramelized.
4. Pour the sauce over the vegetables, and cook for 2-3 minutes, stirring constantly, until the sauce thickens and coats the vegetables.
5. Serve the stir-fry hot, garnished with fresh herbs, if desired.

You can also add other ingredients to the stir-fry, such as grilled chicken, beef, or shrimp, or other types of vegetables, such as zucchini, eggplant, or bok choy, depending on your preference and availability. You can also use different sauces, such as peanut sauce, hoisin sauce, or coconut curry sauce, to add depth and complexity to the flavor of the stir-fry. You can also serve the stir-fry with a side of rice, quinoa, or noodles, to make it more filling and satisfying.

Recipe 3: Quinoa Stir-Fry

This protein-packed stir-fry is made with quinoa, vegetables, and a savory sauce.

Here is a simple and flavorful recipe for quinoa stir-fry that you can enjoy during the Daniel Fast, or any other time:

Ingredients:

- 1 cup quinoa, cooked
- 1 tablespoon olive oil
- 1 cup bell peppers, diced
- 1 cup onions, diced
- 1 cup carrots, sliced
- 1 cup broccoli florets
- 1 cup cherry tomatoes, halved

- 1 cup mushrooms, sliced
- 1 cup snow peas

For the sauce:

- 1/2 cup vegetable broth
- 1/4 cup soy sauce
- 1 tablespoon cornstarch
- 1 teaspoon sesame oil
- 1 teaspoon honey
- 1 clove garlic, minced
- 1 teaspoon ginger, minced
- 1 teaspoon chili flakes (optional)

Instructions:

1. In a small bowl, whisk together the vegetable broth, the soy sauce, the cornstarch, the sesame oil, the honey, the garlic, the ginger, and the chili flakes (if using). Set aside.
2. Heat the olive oil in a large wok or skillet over medium-high heat.
3. Add the bell peppers, the onions, the carrots, the broccoli, the cherry tomatoes, the mushrooms, and the snow peas to the wok, and cook for 5 minutes, stirring occasionally, until they are tender and lightly caramelized.

4. Add the cooked quinoa to the wok, and stir to combine.
5. Pour the sauce over the quinoa and vegetables, and cook for 2-3 minutes, stirring constantly, until the sauce thickens and coats the quinoa and vegetables.
6. Serve the stir-fry hot, garnished with fresh herbs, if desired.

You can also add other ingredients to the stir-fry, such as grilled chicken, beef, or shrimp, or other types of vegetables, such as zucchini, eggplant, or bok choy, depending on your preference and availability. You can also use different sauces, such as peanut sauce, hoisin sauce, or coconut curry sauce, to add depth and complexity to the flavor of the stir-fry. You can also serve the stir-fry with a side of rice, quinoa, or noodles, to make it more filling and satisfying.

PASTA RECIPES

Recipe 1: Spaghetti with Lentil Bolognese

This hearty and satisfying pasta recipe is made with lentils, vegetables, and a savory sauce.

Here is a simple and flavorful recipe for spaghetti with lentil bolognese that you can enjoy during the Daniel Fast, or any other time:

Ingredients:

- 8 ounces spaghetti
- 1 tablespoon olive oil
- 1 cup onions, diced
- 1 cup carrots, diced
- 1 cup celery, diced
- 1 cup mushrooms, sliced
- 1 cup lentils, rinsed and drained
- 1 cup canned crushed tomatoes
- 1 cup tomato sauce
- 1 cup water
- 1 teaspoon dried basil
- 1 teaspoon dried oregano
- 1 teaspoon dried thyme
- 1 teaspoon garlic powder
- Salt and pepper to taste

Instructions:

1. Cook the spaghetti according to the package instructions, and drain. Set aside.
2. Heat the olive oil in a large saucepan over medium heat.

3. Add the onions, the carrots, the celery, and the mushrooms to the saucepan, and cook for 5 minutes, stirring occasionally, until they are tender and fragrant.
4. Add the lentils, the crushed tomatoes, the tomato sauce, the water, the basil, the oregano, the thyme, the garlic powder, and the salt and pepper to the saucepan, and stir to combine.
5. Bring the bolognese to a boil, and reduce the heat to low.
6. Simmer the bolognese for 30 minutes, stirring occasionally, until the lentils are tender and the sauce has thickened.
7. Serve the spaghetti with the lentil bolognese, garnished with fresh herbs, if desired.

You can also add other ingredients to the bolognese, such as ground beef, pork, or turkey, or other types of vegetables, such as bell peppers, zucchini, or eggplant, depending on your preference and availability. You can also use different herbs and spices, such as cumin, paprika, or chili flakes, to add depth and complexity to the flavor of the bolognese. You can also serve the bolognese with a side of garlic bread, or with a salad, to make it more filling and satisfying.

Recipe 2: Fettuccine with Roasted Vegetables

This flavorful and satisfying pasta recipe is made with roasted vegetables, such as bell peppers, onions, and cherry tomatoes, and a creamy sauce.

Here is a simple and flavorful recipe for fettuccine with roasted vegetables that you can enjoy during the Daniel Fast, or any other time:

Ingredients:

- 8 ounces fettuccine
- 1 tablespoon olive oil
- 1 cup bell peppers, sliced
- 1 cup onions, sliced
- 1 cup carrots, sliced
- 1 cup broccoli florets
- 1 cup cherry tomatoes, halved
- 1 cup mushrooms, sliced
- Salt and pepper to taste

For the sauce:

- 1/2 cup vegetable broth
- 1/4 cup soy sauce
- 1 tablespoon cornstarch

- 1 teaspoon sesame oil
- 1 teaspoon honey
- 1 clove garlic, minced
- 1 teaspoon ginger, minced
- 1 teaspoon chili flakes (optional)

Instructions:

1. Cook the fettuccine according to the package instructions, and drain. Set aside.
2. Preheat the oven to 400°F (200°C).
3. In a small bowl, whisk together the vegetable broth, the soy sauce, the cornstarch, the sesame oil, the honey, the garlic, the ginger, and the chili flakes (if using). Set aside.
4. In a large baking sheet, toss the bell peppers, the onions, the carrots, the broccoli, the cherry tomatoes, the mushrooms, the salt, and the pepper with the olive oil.
5. Roast the vegetables in the oven for 20 minutes, or until they are tender and lightly caramelized.
6. In a large saucepan, combine the roasted vegetables and the sauce, and cook for 2-3 minutes, stirring constantly, until the sauce thickens and coats the vegetables.
7. Serve the fettuccine with the roasted vegetables and the sauce, garnished with fresh herbs, if desired.

You can also add other ingredients to the fettuccine, such as grilled chicken, beef, or shrimp, or other types of vegetables, such as zucchini, eggplant, or bok choy, depending on your preference and availability. You can also use different sauces, such as peanut sauce, hoisin sauce, or coconut curry sauce, to add depth and complexity to the flavor of the fettuccine. You can also serve the fettuccine with a side of rice, quinoa, or noodles, to make it more filling and satisfying.

Recipe 3: Penne with White Bean Alfredo

This creamy and satisfying pasta recipe is made with white beans, vegetables, and a rich and flavorful Alfredo sauce.

Here is a simple and flavorful recipe for penne with white bean alfredo that you can enjoy during the Daniel Fast, or any other time:

Ingredients:

- 8 ounces penne
- 1 tablespoon olive oil
- 1 cup onions, diced
- 1 cup garlic, minced
- 1 cup canned white beans, rinsed and drained

- 1 cup vegetable broth
- 1 cup unsweetened almond milk
- 1/2 cup nutritional yeast
- 1 teaspoon dried basil
- 1 teaspoon dried oregano
- 1 teaspoon dried thyme
- Salt and pepper to taste

Instructions:

1. Cook the penne according to the package instructions, and drain. Set aside.
2. Heat the olive oil in a large saucepan over medium heat.
3. Add the onions and the garlic to the saucepan, and cook for 5 minutes, stirring occasionally, until they are tender and fragrant.
4. Add the white beans, the vegetable broth, the almond milk, the nutritional yeast, the basil, the oregano, the thyme, the salt, and the pepper to the saucepan, and stir to combine.
5. Bring the alfredo to a boil, and reduce the heat to low.
6. Simmer the alfredo for 10 minutes, stirring occasionally, until it thickens and becomes creamy.
7. Serve the penne with the white bean alfredo, garnished with fresh herbs, if desired.

You can also add other ingredients to the alfredo, such as grilled chicken, beef, or shrimp, or other types of vegetables, such as bell peppers, zucchini, or eggplant, depending on your preference and availability. You can also use different herbs and spices, such as cumin, paprika, or chili flakes, to add depth and complexity to the flavor of the alfredo. You can also serve the alfredo with a side of garlic bread, or with a salad, to make it more filling and satisfying.

CHAPTER FIVE

[Snacks and Desserts: Recipes for healthy snacks and sweet treats that are suitable for the Daniel Fast.]

INTRODUCTION TO DESSERT RECIPES FOR THE DANIEL FAST

As you embark on the Daniel Fast, it's natural to crave something sweet and indulgent every now and then. In this chapter, you'll find a variety of dessert recipes that are suitable for the Daniel Fast and that will help you satisfy your sweet tooth without overdoing it. Each recipe includes a list of ingredients, step-by-step instructions, and nutritional information to help you plan and prepare your desserts.

Ideas For Indulging In Dessert Without Overdoing It

Here are some ideas for indulging in dessert without overdoing it, that you can consider during the Daniel Fast, or any other time:

1. Choose small portion sizes: Instead of having a large slice of cake, opt for a smaller portion, such as a single cookie, a mini cupcake, or a small piece of fruit. This will allow you to satisfy your sweet tooth without consuming too many calories or sugar.

2. Choose healthier options: Instead of having sugary, processed desserts, opt for healthier options, such as fresh fruit, smoothies, yogurt, or frozen yogurt. These options are typically lower in sugar and calories, and they also provide important nutrients, such as fiber, vitamins, and minerals.

3. Practice moderation: Instead of having dessert every day, or multiple times a day, practice moderation, and limit your intake to a few times a week. This will allow you to enjoy dessert without feeling guilty, and without compromising your health goals.

4. Make your own desserts: Instead of buying pre-packaged desserts, try making your own desserts at home, using whole, natural ingredients, such as fruits, nuts, seeds, whole grains, and spices. This will allow you to control the quality and the quantity of the ingredients, and to customize the flavor and the sweetness to your preference.

5. Choose low-sugar alternatives: Instead of using regular sugar, opt for low-sugar alternatives, such as stevia, erythritol, or monk fruit, which have a lower

glycemic index and are less likely to spike your blood sugar. You can also use fruit puree, such as applesauce or mashed bananas, as a natural sweetener in your desserts.

Tips For Choosing And Preparing Desserts That Are Suitable For The Daniel Fast

FRUIT-BASED RECIPES

Recipe 1: Grilled Pineapple with Coconut Whip

Ingredients:

- 1 pineapple, peeled and sliced
- 1 tbsp of coconut oil or vegetable oil
- 1 cup of coconut cream
- 2 tbsp of honey or maple syrup
- 1 tsp of vanilla extract
- 1/4 tsp of salt

Instructions:

1. Preheat a grill or a grill pan over medium heat.
2. Brush the pineapple slices with coconut oil or vegetable oil.
3. Grill the pineapple slices for 2-3 minutes on each side, or until they are lightly charred and tender.
4. Transfer the grilled pineapple to a plate, and let it cool slightly.
5. In a large bowl, beat the coconut cream, honey or maple syrup, vanilla extract, and salt together until soft peaks form.
6. Serve the grilled pineapple with a dollop of coconut whip on top, or alongside the coconut whip in a separate bowl.

This grilled pineapple with coconut whip is a delicious and tropical dessert option for the Daniel Fast, as it is made with natural and healthy ingredients, and it provides a good source of fiber, vitamins, and minerals. You can customize this recipe by adding a sprinkle of chopped nuts or seeds, or a drizzle of chocolate sauce, on top of the coconut whip, or by using a different type of sweetener, such as agave nectar or coconut sugar. You can also make this dessert vegan by using maple syrup instead of honey, and by using a plant-based whipping cream instead of coconut cream. Enjoy!

Recipe 2: Baked Apples with Oatmeal Streusel

Ingredients:

- 4 apples, cored and sliced
- 1 cup of rolled oats
- 1/2 cup of almond flour
- 1/4 cup of coconut oil or butter
- 1/4 cup of honey or maple syrup
- 1 tsp of cinnamon
- 1/2 tsp of nutmeg
- 1/4 tsp of allspice
- 1/4 tsp of salt

Instructions:

1. Preheat the oven to 350°F (180°C).
2. Arrange the apple slices in a baking dish or individual serving cups.
3. In a small bowl, mix together the oats, almond flour, coconut oil or butter, honey or maple syrup, cinnamon, nutmeg, allspice, and salt until a crumbly mixture forms.
4. Sprinkle the oatmeal streusel over the apple slices.
5. Bake the apples for 20-25 minutes, or until they are tender and the streusel is golden brown.

6. Serve the baked apples warm, garnished with a drizzle of honey or maple syrup, or a sprinkle of chopped nuts or seeds.

These baked apples with oatmeal streusel are a delicious and comforting dessert option for the Daniel Fast, as they are made with wholesome and natural ingredients, and they provide a good source of fiber, vitamins, and minerals. You can customize this recipe by using different types of apples, or by adding a pinch of spices, such as ginger or cardamom, or a sprinkle of herbs, such as rosemary or thyme, to the streusel mixture. You can also make this dessert vegan by using maple syrup instead of honey, and by using a plant-based butter instead of regular butter. Enjoy!

Recipe 3: Banana Ice Cream

Ingredients:

- 4 bananas, peeled and frozen
- 1/4 cup of almond milk or coconut milk
- 2 tbsps. of honey or maple syrup
- 1 tsp. of vanilla extract
- 1/4 tsp. of salt

Instructions:

1. In a blender or food processor, blend the frozen bananas, almond milk or coconut milk, honey or maple syrup, vanilla extract, and salt until smooth and creamy.
2. Pour the banana mixture into a loaf pan or a silicone mold, and freeze for at least 4 hours, or until firm.
3. To serve the banana ice cream, scoop it into bowls or cones, and garnish it with a sprinkle of chopped nuts or seeds, or a drizzle of chocolate sauce.

This banana ice cream is a healthy and delicious dessert option for the Daniel Fast, as it is made with natural and whole ingredients, and it provides a good source of fiber, vitamins, and minerals. You can customize this recipe by adding a pinch of spices, such as cinnamon or ginger, or a sprinkle of herbs, such as mint or basil, to the banana mixture, or by using a different type of sweetener, such as agave nectar or coconut sugar. You can also make this ice cream vegan by using maple syrup instead of honey, and by using a plant-based milk instead of dairy milk. Enjoy!

Fruit Salad with Honey Lemon Dressing:

This refreshing and colorful salad is made with a variety of seasonal fruits, and it is dressed with a simple and sweet honey lemon dressing. To make this recipe, you will need the following ingredients:

Ingredients:

- 4 cups of mixed fruits (such as apples, bananas, berries, kiwis, mangoes, or peaches)
- 2 tbsp. of honey
- 1 tbsp. of lemon juice
- 1 tbsp. of water

Instructions:

1. Wash and chop the fruit into bite-sized pieces. Transfer the fruit to a large bowl.
2. In a small bowl, whisk together the honey, lemon juice, and water until well combined.
3. Pour the honey lemon dressing over the fruit in the bowl, and toss everything together until the fruit is well coated.
4. Serve the fruit salad chilled, garnished with a sprinkle of chopped nuts or seeds, or a drizzle of coconut cream.

This fruit salad is a healthy and satisfying dessert option for the Daniel Fast, as it is made with fresh and natural ingredients, and it provides a good source of fiber, vitamins, and minerals. You can customize this recipe by using different types of fruit, depending on what is in season, or by adding a pinch of spices, such as cinnamon or ginger, or a sprinkle of herbs, such as mint or basil. You can also make this salad vegan by using agave nectar or coconut nectar instead of honey. Enjoy!

VEGAN CHOCOLATE RECIPES

Recipe 1: Chocolate Pudding

This rich and creamy pudding is made with tofu, cocoa powder, and a sweetener, and it is a great way to satisfy your chocolate cravings without breaking the Daniel Fast.

Here is a simple and delicious recipe for chocolate pudding that you can enjoy during the Daniel Fast, or any other time:

Ingredients:

- 2 cups unsweetened almond milk
- 1/2 cup cocoa powder
- 1/2 cup cornstarch

- 1/2 cup sugar
- 1/4 teaspoon salt
- 1 teaspoon vanilla extract
- Optional toppings: whipped cream, chocolate chips, nuts, fruit, sprinkles

Instructions:

1. In a medium saucepan, whisk together the almond milk, the cocoa powder, the cornstarch, the sugar, and the salt.
2. Place the saucepan over medium heat, and cook the pudding, stirring constantly, until it thickens and boils.
3. Reduce the heat to low, and simmer the pudding for 2 minutes, stirring constantly, until it becomes smooth and creamy.
4. Remove the saucepan from the heat, and stir in the vanilla extract.
5. Pour the pudding into individual serving cups or bowls, and refrigerate for at least 2 hours, or until it sets.
6. Serve the pudding chilled, with your choice of toppings, such as whipped cream, chocolate chips, nuts, fruit, or sprinkles.

You can also add other ingredients to the pudding, such as peanut butter, coconut milk, or coffee, to add depth and complexity to the flavor. You can also use different sweeteners, such as honey, maple syrup, or agave nectar, to adjust the sweetness to your preference. You can also use different types of chocolate, such as dark chocolate, milk chocolate, or white chocolate, to vary the intensity of the flavor.

Recipe 2: Chocolate Truffles

These indulgent and rich truffles are made with dates, nuts, cocoa powder, and a touch of coconut oil, and they are a perfect guilt-free treat for the Daniel Fast.

Here is a simple and indulging recipe for chocolate truffles that you can enjoy during the Daniel Fast, or any other time:

Ingredients:

- 8 ounces chocolate chips
- 1/2 cup heavy cream
- 1 tablespoon butter
- Optional coatings: cocoa powder, powdered sugar, sprinkles, nuts, coconut flakes

Instructions:

1. In a medium saucepan, heat the chocolate chips, the heavy cream, and the butter over medium heat, stirring constantly, until the chocolate is melted and the mixture is smooth.
2. Remove the saucepan from the heat, and let the truffle mixture cool for 10 minutes.
3. Scoop the truffle mixture using a small cookie scoop, or a spoon, and roll it into small balls using your hands.
4. Place the truffles on a baking sheet lined with parchment paper, and refrigerate for at least 2 hours, or until they set.
5. Roll the truffles in your choice of coatings, such as cocoa powder, powdered sugar, sprinkles, nuts, or coconut flakes.
6. Serve the truffles chilled, as a indulging and satisfying dessert.

You can also add other ingredients to the truffles, such as peanut butter, coconut milk, or coffee, to add depth and complexity to the flavor. You can also use different types of chocolate, such as dark chocolate, milk chocolate, or white chocolate, to vary the intensity of the flavor. You can also use different sweeteners, such as honey, maple syrup, or agave nectar, to adjust the sweetness to your preference.

Recipe 3: Chocolate Mousse

This light and fluffy mousse is made with avocado, cocoa powder, and a sweetener, and it is a healthy and satisfying way to satisfy your chocolate cravings.

Here is a simple and indulging recipe for chocolate mousse that you can enjoy during the Daniel Fast, or any other time:

Ingredients:

- 8 ounces chocolate chips
- 1 cup heavy cream
- 2 egg whites
- 2 tablespoons sugar
- 1 teaspoon vanilla extract
- Optional toppings: whipped cream, chocolate chips, nuts, fruit, sprinkles

Instructions:

1. In a medium saucepan, heat the chocolate chips and 1/2 cup of the heavy cream over medium heat, stirring constantly, until the chocolate is melted and the mixture is smooth.

2. Remove the saucepan from the heat, and let the chocolate mixture cool for 10 minutes.

3. In a medium bowl, beat the egg whites using an electric mixer, until they form soft peaks.

4. Gradually add the sugar to the egg whites, and continue beating until the meringue is stiff and glossy.

5. In a separate medium bowl, beat the remaining 1/2 cup of heavy cream using an electric mixer, until it forms stiff peaks.

6. Gently fold the chocolate mixture, the meringue, and the whipped cream together, using a spatula, until they are well combined.

7. Spoon the mousse into individual serving cups or bowls, and refrigerates for at least 2 hours, or until it sets.

8. Serve the mousse chilled, with your choice of toppings, such as whipped cream, chocolate chips, nuts, fruit, or sprinkles.

You can also add other ingredients to the mousse, such as peanut butter, coconut milk, or coffee, to add depth and complexity to the flavor. You can also use different types of chocolate, such as dark chocolate, milk chocolate, or white chocolate, to vary the intensity of the flavor. You can also use different sweeteners, such as honey, maple syrup, or agave nectar, to adjust the sweetness to your preference.

NO-BAKE RECIPES

Recipe 1: No-Bake Cheesecake

This creamy and indulgent cheesecake is made with soaked cashews, coconut cream, and a touch of lemon juice, and it requires no baking at all.

Here is a simple and indulging recipe for no-bake cheesecake that you can enjoy during the Daniel Fast, or any other time:

Ingredients:

- 1 1/2 cups graham cracker crumbs
- 6 tablespoons butter, melted
- 24 ounces cream cheese, softened
- 1 cup sugar
- 1 cup heavy cream
- 2 tablespoons lemon juice
- 1 teaspoon vanilla extract
- Optional toppings: whipped cream, fruit, chocolate chips, nuts, sprinkles

Instructions:

1. In a medium bowl, mix the graham cracker crumbs and the melted butter together, using a fork, until the mixture is well combined.
2. Press the graham cracker mixture into the bottom of a 9-inch springform pan, and refrigerate for at least 15 minutes, or until it sets.
3. In a large bowl, beat the cream cheese and the sugar together, using an electric mixer, until the mixture is smooth and creamy.
4. In a separate medium bowl, beat the heavy cream until it forms stiff peaks.
5. Gently fold the whipped cream, the lemon juice, and the vanilla extract into the cream cheese mixture, using a spatula, until they are well combined.
6. Pour the cheesecake mixture over the graham cracker crust, and smooth the top with a spatula.
7. Refrigerate the cheesecake for at least 4 hours, or until it sets.
8. Serve the cheesecake chilled, with your choice of toppings, such as whipped cream, fruit, chocolate chips, nuts, or sprinkles.

You can also add other ingredients to the cheesecake, such as peanut butter, coconut milk, or coffee, to add depth and complexity to the flavor. You can also use different types of cookies or crackers for the crust, such as vanilla wafers, Oreos, or animal crackers, to vary the texture and the flavor. You can also use different sweeteners, such as honey, maple syrup, or agave nectar, to adjust the sweetness to your preference.

Recipe 2: No-Bake Oat Bars

These chewy and satisfying bars are made with oats, nuts, dates, and a touch of coconut oil, and they require no baking at all.

Here is a simple and nourishing recipe for no-bake oat bars that you can enjoy during the Daniel Fast, or any other time:

Ingredients:

- 2 cups rolled oats
- 1/2 cup peanut butter
- 1/2 cup honey
- 1/2 cup unsweetened coconut flakes
- 1/2 cup chocolate chips
- Optional mix-ins: nuts, dried fruit, spices, coconut oil, cocoa powder

Instructions:

1. Line an 8-inch square baking pan with parchment paper, and set it aside.
2. In a medium saucepan, heat the peanut butter and the honey over medium heat, stirring constantly, until they are melted and well combined.
3. Remove the saucepan from the heat, and stir in the oats, the coconut flakes, and the chocolate chips, until they are well coated with the peanut butter mixture.
4. Stir in your choice of mix-ins, such as nuts, dried fruit, spices, coconut oil, or cocoa powder.
5. Press the oat mixture into the prepared baking pan, and smooth the top with a spatula.
6. Refrigerate the oat bars for at least 2 hours, or until they set.
7. Cut the oat bars into squares, and serve.

You can also add other ingredients to the oat bars, such as almond butter, cashew butter, or sunflower seed butter, to vary the flavor and the texture. You can also use different types of oats, such as quick oats, steel-cut oats, or old-fashioned oats, to vary the texture and the flavor. You can also use different sweeteners, such as maple syrup, agave nectar, or brown rice syrup, to adjust the sweetness to your preference.

Recipe 3: No-Bake Peanut Butter Cookies

These soft and chewy cookies are made with oats, peanut butter, and a sweetener, and they require no baking at all.

Here is a simple and indulging recipe for no-bake peanut butter cookies that you can enjoy during the Daniel Fast, or any other time:

Ingredients:

- 1 cup peanut butter
- 1 cup sugar
- 1 egg
- 1 teaspoon vanilla extract
- Optional toppings: chocolate chips, nuts, coconut flakes, sprinkles

Instructions:

1. In a medium bowl, mix the peanut butter, the sugar, the egg, and the vanilla extract together, using a fork, until the mixture is well combined.
2. Shape the peanut butter mixture into small balls, using your hands or a small cookie scoop.
3. Place the peanut butter balls on a baking sheet lined with parchment paper, and flatten them

slightly with a fork, making a crisscross pattern on top.

4. Top the peanut butter cookies with your choice of toppings, such as chocolate chips, nuts, coconut flakes, or sprinkles.

5. Refrigerate the peanut butter cookies for at least 1 hour, or until they set.

6. Serve the peanut butter cookies chilled, or store them in an airtight container in the fridge for up to 1 week.

You can also add other ingredients to the peanut butter cookies, such as oats, coconut, or cocoa powder, to add depth and complexity to the flavor. You can also use different types of nut butters, such as almond butter, cashew butter, or sunflower seed butter, to vary the flavor and the texture. You can also use different sweeteners, such as honey, maple syrup, or agave nectar, to adjust the sweetness to your preference.

No-Bake Energy Bars:

These tasty and nourishing bars are made with oats, nuts, seeds, dried fruit, and a touch of honey, and they are a perfect snack or breakfast option for the Daniel Fast.

To make this recipe, you will need the following ingredients:

- 2 cups of oats
- 1 cup of nuts (such as almonds, walnuts, or pecans)
- 1 cup of seeds (such as sunflower seeds, pumpkin seeds, or chia seeds)
- 1 cup of dried fruit (such as raisins, dates, or apricots)
- 1/2 cup of honey or maple syrup
- 1/4 cup of coconut oil or nut butter
- 1 tsp of vanilla extract
- 1/4 tsp of salt

Instructions:

1. In a food processor or blender, process the oats until they are ground into flour. Transfer the oat flour to a large bowl.
2. In the same food processor or blender, process the nuts until they are finely ground. Transfer the ground nuts to the bowl with the oat flour.
3. In the same food processor or blender, process the seeds until they are finely ground. Transfer the ground seeds to the bowl with the oat flour and nuts.

4. In the same food processor or blender, process the dried fruit until it is finely chopped. Transfer the chopped dried fruit to the bowl with the oats, nuts, and seeds.

5. In a small saucepan, melt the honey or maple syrup, coconut oil or nut butter, and vanilla extract over low heat, stirring constantly, until the mixture is smooth and well combined.

6. Pour the honey mixture over the oats, nuts, seeds, and dried fruit in the bowl, and mix everything together until the ingredients are well coated.

7. Press the mixture into a 9x9-inch baking dish lined with parchment paper, or into individual serving cups or molds.

8. Refrigerate the energy bars for at least 1 hour, or until firm, then cut them into squares or slice them and serve them chilled.

These no-bake energy bars are a delicious and nutritious snack or breakfast option for the Daniel Fast, as they are packed with oats, nuts, seeds, and dried fruit, which provide a good source of fiber, protein, healthy fats, and vitamins and minerals. You can customize this recipe by using different types of oats, nuts, seeds, and dried fruit, or by adding a pinch of spices, such as cinnamon or ginger, or a sprinkle of cocoa powder or chocolate chips.

You can also make these energy bars vegan by using maple syrup instead of honey, and by using coconut oil or a plant-based butter instead of regular butter. Enjoy!

CHAPTER SIX

[Meal Planning and Prep: Tips and resources to help you plan and prepare your meals, including a suggested meal plan, grocery list, and pantry essentials.]

MEAL PLANNING AND PREP

Meal planning and prep are essential components of a successful and sustainable Daniel Fast, as they help you to save time, money, and stress, and to stay focused and motivated on your fast. By planning and preparing your meals in advance, you can ensure that you have a variety of healthy and delicious options available to you, and that you are able to stick to your fast, even when you are busy or faced with challenges or temptations.

Here Are Some Tips And Resources To Help You Plan And Prepare Your Meals For The Daniel Fast:

- **Choose a meal plan:** There are many different meal plans available for the Daniel Fast, depending on your goals, preferences, and needs. Some common meal plans for the Daniel Fast include the standard Daniel Fast, which consists of fruits, vegetables, whole grains, legumes, nuts, and seeds, and excludes animal products, dairy products, processed foods, and sweeteners; the modified Daniel Fast, which allows for some animal products and dairy products in moderation; and the vegan Daniel Fast, which excludes all animal products, and relies on plant-based sources of protein, such as legumes, nuts, and seeds. You can choose a meal plan that works best for you, or you can create your own meal plan by mixing and matching different foods and ingredients that are allowed on the Daniel Fast. Plan your meals in advance, by creating a meal plan that covers all your meals and snacks for the duration of the Daniel Fast. A meal plan will help you to organize your meals, to save time and money, and to avoid impulse eating or snacking.

- **Make a grocery list:** Once you have chosen a meal plan, you can make a grocery list of all the ingredients and supplies you will need for your meals. To make a comprehensive grocery list, you can refer to your meal plan, and to your pantry and fridge, and you can write down all the items that you need to buy or restock. You can also use a grocery list template or app to help you organize and prioritize your items. A grocery list will help you to shop efficiently, to avoid unnecessary or unhealthy purchases, and to save money.

- **Stock your pantry:** Your pantry is a key resource for your meal planning and prep, as it is where you store all your non-perishable and shelf-stable ingredients and supplies. To stock your pantry for the Daniel Fast, you can purchase a variety of whole grains, legumes, nuts, seeds, dried fruit, canned or boxed goods, and spices, that are allowed on the Daniel Fast, and that can be used to prepare a variety of dishes and snacks. You can also invest in some pantry essentials, such as storage containers, containers, bags, and wraps, to help you store and transport your food safely and easily.

- **Prepare in advance:** Prepare your meals and snacks in advance, whenever possible, by cooking and freezing large batches of food, or by prepping ingredients ahead of time. Preparing in advance will save you time and effort during the week, and will make it easier for you to follow your meal plan.

- **Use resources:** Use resources, such as cookbooks, websites, apps, or social media, to find inspiration and guidance for your meals and snacks. Resources can provide you with recipes, tips, and ideas that can help you to plan and prepare your meals in a creative and enjoyable way.

SUGGESTED 7-DAY MEAL PLAN:

Here is a suggested meal plan for the Daniel Fast that you can use as a guide:

Day 1:

- Breakfast: Overnight oats with banana, berries, and nuts
- Lunch: Kale salad with quinoa, roasted vegetables, and tahini dressing
- Dinner: Spaghetti with lentil Bolognese and garlic bread

Day 2:

- Breakfast: Green smoothie with spinach, banana, and almond milk
- Lunch: Grilled eggplant sandwiches with hummus and tomato
- Dinner: Vegetable stir-fry with tofu and quinoa

Day 3:

- Breakfast: Banana nut oatmeal with raisins and almonds
- Lunch: Tomato soup with grilled cheese sandwiches
- Dinner: Grilled Portobello mushrooms with roasted potatoes and steamed broccoli

Day 4:

- Breakfast: Acai bowl with granola and fruit
- Lunch: Quinoa salad with avocado, corn, and black beans
- Dinner: Baked apples with oatmeal streusel and vanilla ice cream

Day 5:

- Breakfast: Smoothie bowl with mango, spinach, and coconut milk
- Lunch: Black bean soup with cornbread
- Dinner: Grilled zucchini with quinoa and roasted chickpeas

Day 6:

- Breakfast: Chocolate pudding with whipped cream and berries
- Lunch: Caesar salad with grilled chicken and croutons
- Dinner: Penne with white bean Alfred and steamed asparagus

Day 7:

- Breakfast: Peanut butter granola with milk and fruit

- Lunch: Butternut squash soup with grilled cheese sandwiches
- Dinner: Fettuccine with roasted vegetables and garlic bread

You can customize this meal plan to your personal preferences and dietary needs, by adding or replacing meals and ingredients that suit your taste and your health. You can also experiment with different recipes, and try new foods and flavors, to make the Daniel Fast a satisfying and enjoyable experience.

SUGGESTED GROCERY LIST:

Here is a suggested grocery list for the Daniel Fast that you can use as a guide:

Produce:

- Bananas
- Berries (strawberries, blueberries, raspberries)
- Spinach
- Kale
- Mixed vegetables (bell peppers, onions, zucchini, eggplant, broccoli, carrots)
- Avocado
- Tomato
- Corn

- Black beans
- Apples
- Mango
- Garlic
- Potatoes
- Asparagus
- Chickpeas
- Lentils

Protein:

- Tofu
- Chicken breasts
- Hummus
- Peanut butter
- Almond butter
- Cashew butter

Grains:

- Rolled oats
- Whole wheat flour
- Whole wheat pasta
- Quinoa
- Cornmeal

Dairy:

- Milk

- Almond milk
- Coconut milk
- Cream
- Cheese
- Butter

Nuts/Seeds:

- Nuts (almonds, walnuts, peanuts)
- Coconut flakes
- Chia seeds
- Flax seeds

Spices/Seasonings:

- Salt
- Pepper
- Garlic powder
- Onion powder
- Paprika
- Chili powder
- Oregano
- Basil
- Thyme

Sweeteners:

- Sugar
- Honey

- Maple syrup
- Brown sugar

Other:

- Vanilla extract
- Baking powder
- Baking soda
- Olive oil
- Coconut oil
- Apple cider vinegar
- Lemon juice
- Tahini
- Peanut butter
- Chocolate chips
- Sprinkles
- Coconut flakes

You can customize this grocery list to your personal preferences and dietary needs, by adding or replacing items that suit your taste and your health. You can also consider buying organic, local, or seasonal products, to support sustainable and responsible agriculture.

SUGGESTED PANTRY ESSENTIALS:

Here are some suggested pantry essentials for the Daniel Fast that you can use as a guide:

- Canned goods: tomatoes, beans, corn, coconut milk, broth
- Grains: oats, quinoa, pasta, rice, flour
- Legumes: lentils, chickpeas, kidney beans, black beans
- Nuts/seeds: almonds, walnuts, peanuts, chia seeds, flax seeds, pumpkin seeds
- Sweeteners: honey, maple syrup, brown sugar
- Spices/seasonings: salt, pepper, garlic powder, onion powder, paprika, chili powder, oregano, basil, thyme
- Condiments: peanut butter, almond butter, tahini, soy sauce, hot sauce, salsa, olive oil, coconut oil, vinegar, lemon juice
- Baking supplies: baking powder, baking soda, cocoa powder
- Other: vanilla extract, chocolate chips, coconut flakes, sprinkles

You can customize this list to your personal preferences and dietary needs, by adding or replacing items that suit your taste and your health. You can also consider buying organic, non-GMO, or gluten-free products, to support your dietary preferences and requirements.

CHAPTER SEVEN

[Incorporating Prayer and Bible Study: Ideas for incorporating prayer and Bible study into your daily routine during the Daniel Fast.]

INCORPORATING PRAYER AND BIBLE STUDY

The focus of the Daniel Fast is prayer. While it's natural to be concerned about the food list, your priority on the fast should always be calling out to God on behalf of your own needs and the needs of others. Therefore, setting aside dedicated time for bible reading, prayer, and fasting is a great undertaking and one to be taken seriously. Jesus himself has told us in Mark 9 and Matthew 17 that some things can only be accomplished through both prayer *and* fasting.

Prayer and Bible study are integral parts of the Daniel Fast, as they provide a spiritual foundation and guidance for your fast, and they enable you to connect with God, and to seek His will and wisdom. By incorporating prayer and Bible study into your daily routine during the Daniel Fast, you can deepen your relationship with God, and you can gain a greater understanding and appreciation of His Word and His ways.

Here are some ideas for incorporating prayer and Bible study into your daily routine during the Daniel Fast:

- **Set aside a dedicated time and place for prayer and Bible study:** To make the most of your prayer and Bible study time, you can set aside a dedicated time and place for these activities, such as early in the morning, before you start your day, or late at night, before you go to bed. You can also choose a quiet and comfortable spot, such as a room, a corner, or a park, where you can focus and relax, and where you can avoid distractions and interruptions.

- **Use a prayer journal or Bible study guide:** To help you organize and reflect on your prayer and Bible study sessions, you can use a prayer journal or Bible study guide. A prayer journal is a notebook or a planner where you can write down your prayers, your thoughts, your feelings, and your responses to God. A Bible study guide is a manual or a workbook that provides questions, comments, and insights on a specific passage or theme of the Bible. You can use a prayer journal or Bible study guide that suits your style and needs, and that helps you to engage and apply the Word of God to your life.

- **Join a prayer or Bible study group:** To enrich and support your prayer and Bible study experience, you can join a prayer or Bible study group. A prayer or Bible study group is a community of believers who meet regularly to pray and study the Bible together. You can find a prayer or Bible study group in your church, your neighborhood, or online, and you can participate in the group's activities and discussions, and you can share your insights and experiences with others.

- **Use resources and tools:** To enhance and expand your prayer and Bible study time, you can use resources and tools that are available to you. Some resources and tools that you can use include a Bible app or website, a devotional book or podcast, a commentary or a dictionary, a prayer or worship song, or a video or an audio message. You can use these resources and tools to help you access and understand the Bible, to stimulate your prayer and worship, and to enrich your spiritual growth.

SUGGESTED 21 SCRIPTURE READINGS TO USE DURING YOUR FAST

If you're considering the 21 day Daniel Fast, these daily **Daniel Fast scripture readings** and bible reading plan will help you be consistent with your time spent in the Word. Spend time in God's word each day, and then pause to reflect on what you've read.

DAY 1
Daniel 9:3-4

[3] And I set my face unto the Lord God, to seek by prayer and supplications, with fasting, and sackcloth, and ashes:

[4] And I prayed unto the Lord my God, and made my confession, and said, O Lord, the great and dreadful God, keeping the covenant and mercy to them that love him, and to them that keep his commandments.

DAY 2
Daniel 9:5

We have sinned, and have committed iniquity, and have done wickedly, and have rebelled, even by departing from thy precepts and from thy judgments:

DAY 3
Daniel 9:17-19

[17] Now therefore, O our God, hear the prayer of thy servant, and his supplications, and cause thy face to

shine upon thy sanctuary that is desolate, for the Lord's sake.

[18] O my God, incline thine ear, and hear; open thine eyes, and behold our desolations, and the city which is called by thy name: for we do not present our supplications before thee for our righteousness', but for thy great mercies.

[19] O Lord, hear; O Lord, forgive; O Lord, hearken and do; defer not, for thine own sake, O my God: for thy city and thy people are called by thy name.

DAY 4
Daniel 1:11-14

[11] Then said Daniel to Melzar, whom the prince of the eunuchs had set over Daniel, Hananiah, Mishael, and Azariah,

[12] Prove thy servants, I beseech thee, ten days; and let them give us pulse to eat, and water to drink.

[13] Then let our countenances be looked upon before thee, and the countenance of the children that eat of the portion of the king's meat: and as thou seest, deal with thy servants.

[14] So he consented to them in this matter, and proved them ten days.

DAY 5
Daniel 10:1-3

[1] In the third year of Cyrus king of Persia a thing was revealed unto Daniel, whose name was called Belteshazzar; and the thing [was] true, but the time appointed [was] long: and he understood the thing, and had understanding of the vision.

[2] In those days I Daniel was mourning three full weeks.

[3] I ate no pleasant bread, neither came flesh nor wine in my mouth, neither did I anoint myself at all, till three whole weeks were fulfilled.

DAY 6
Daniel 10:4-7

[4] And in the four and twentieth day of the first month, as I was by the side of the great river, which [is] Hiddekel;

⁵ Then I lifted up mine eyes, and looked, and behold a certain man clothed in linen, whose loins [were] girded with fine gold of Uphaz:

⁶ His body also [was] like the beryl, and his face as the appearance of lightning, and his eyes as lamps of fire, and his arms and his feet like in colour to polished brass, and the voice of his words like the voice of a multitude.

⁷ And I Daniel alone saw the vision: for the men that were with me saw not the vision; but a great quaking fell upon them, so that they fled to hide themselves.

DAY 7
Daniel 10:8-11

⁸ Therefore I was left alone, and saw this great vision, and there remained no strength in me: for my comeliness was turned in me into corruption, and I retained no strength.

⁹ Yet heard I the voice of his words: and when I heard the voice of his words, then was I in a deep sleep on my face, and my face toward the ground.

¹⁰ And, behold, an hand touched me, which set me upon my knees and [upon] the palms of my hands.

[11] And he said unto me, O Daniel, a man greatly beloved, understand the words that I speak unto thee, and stand upright: for unto thee am I now sent. And when he had spoken this word unto me, I stood trembling.

DAY 8
Daniel 10:12-15

[12] Then said he unto me, Fear not, Daniel: for from the first day that thou didst set thine heart to understand and to chasten thyself before thy God, thy words were heard, and I am come for thy words.

[13] But the prince of the kingdom of Persia withstood me one and twenty days: but, lo, Michael, one of the chief princes, came to help me; and I remained there with the kings of Persia.

[14] Now I am come to make thee understand what shall befall thy people in the latter days: for yet the vision [is] for [many] days.

[15] And when he had spoken such words unto me, I set my face toward the ground, and I became dumb.

DAY 9
Daniel 10:16-19

¹⁶ And, behold, [one] like the similitude of the sons of men touched my lips: then I opened my mouth, and spake, and said unto him that stood before me, O my lord, by the vision my sorrows are turned upon me, and I have retained no strength.

¹⁷ For how can the servant of this my lord talk with this my lord? For as for me, straightway there remained no strength in me, neither is there breath left in me.

¹⁸ Then there came again and touched me [one] like the appearance of a man, and he strengthened me,

¹⁹ And said, O man greatly beloved, fear not: peace [be] unto thee, be strong, yea, be strong. And when he had spoken unto me, I was strengthened, and said, Let my lord speak; for thou hast strengthened me.

DAY 10
Deuteronomy 28:1-6

And it shall come to pass, if thou shalt hearken diligently unto the voice of the Lord thy God, to observe and to do all his commandments which I command thee this day, that the Lord thy God will set thee on high above all nations of the earth:

2 And all these blessings shall come on thee, and overtake thee, if thou shalt hearken unto the voice of the Lord thy God.

3 Blessed shalt thou be in the city, and blessed shalt thou be in the field.

4 Blessed shall be the fruit of thy body, and the fruit of thy ground, and the fruit of thy cattle, the increase of thy kine, and the flocks of thy sheep.

5 Blessed shall be thy basket and thy store.

6 Blessed shalt thou be when thou comest in, and blessed shalt thou be when thou goest out.

DAY 11
Romans 5:8-9

8 But God commendeth his love toward us, in that, while we were yet sinners, Christ died for us.

⁹ Much more then, being now justified by his blood, we shall be saved from wrath through him.

DAY 12
Psalm 119:97-103

⁹⁷ O how love I thy law! it is my meditation all the day.

⁹⁸ Thou through thy commandments hast made me wiser than mine enemies: for they are ever with me.

⁹⁹ I have more understanding than all my teachers: for thy testimonies are my meditation.

¹⁰⁰ I understand more than the ancients, because I keep thy precepts.

¹⁰¹ I have refrained my feet from every evil way, that I might keep thy word.

¹⁰² I have not departed from thy judgments: for thou hast taught me.

¹⁰³ How sweet are thy words unto my taste! yea, sweeter than honey to my mouth!

DAY 13
Psalm 51:7-10

⁷ Purge me with hyssop, and I shall be clean: wash me, and I shall be whiter than snow.

⁸ Make me to hear joy and gladness; that the bones which thou hast broken may rejoice.

⁹ Hide thy face from my sins, and blot out all mine iniquities.

¹⁰ Create in me a clean heart, O God; and renew a right spirit within me.

DAY 14
Daniel 10:7-12

⁷ And I Daniel alone saw the vision: for the men that were with me saw not the vision; but a great quaking fell upon them, so that they fled to hide themselves.

⁸ Therefore I was left alone, and saw this great vision, and there remained no strength in me: for my comeliness was turned in me into corruption, and I retained no strength.

9 Yet heard I the voice of his words: and when I heard the voice of his words, then was I in a deep sleep on my face, and my face toward the ground.

10 And, behold, an hand touched me, which set me upon my knees and [upon] the palms of my hands.

11 And he said unto me, O Daniel, a man greatly beloved, understand the words that I speak unto thee, and stand upright: for unto thee am I now sent. And when he had spoken this word unto me, I stood trembling.

12 Then said he unto me, Fear not, Daniel: for from the first day that thou didst set thine heart to understand, and to chasten thyself before thy God, thy words were heard, and I am come for thy words.

DAY 15
Mark 16:15-16

15 And he said unto them, Go ye into all the world, and preach the gospel to every creature.

16 He that believeth and is baptized shall be saved; but he that believeth not shall be damned.

DAY 16
2 Chronicles 7:13-14

[13] If I shut up heaven that there be no rain, or if I command the locusts to devour the land, or if I send pestilence among my people;

[14] If my people, which are called by my name, shall humble themselves, and pray, and seek my face, and turn from their wicked ways; then will I hear from heaven, and will forgive their sin, and will heal their land.

DAY 17
Acts 2:1-4

And when the day of Pentecost was fully come, they were all with one accord in one place.

[2] And suddenly there came a sound from heaven as of a rushing mighty wind, and it filled all the house where they were sitting.

[3] And there appeared unto them cloven tongues like as of fire, and it sat upon each of them.

⁴ And they were all filled with the Holy Ghost, and began to speak with other tongues, as the Spirit gave them utterance.

DAY 18
John 3:30-31

³⁰ He must increase, but I must decrease.

³¹ He that cometh from above is above all: he that is of the earth is earthly, and speaketh of the earth: he that cometh from heaven is above all.

DAY 19
Philippians 4:4-8

⁴ Rejoice in the Lord always: and again I say, Rejoice.

⁵ Let your moderation be known unto all men. The Lord is at hand.

⁶ Be careful for nothing; but in everything by prayer and supplication with thanksgiving let your requests be made known unto God.

⁷ And the peace of God, which passeth all understanding, shall keep your hearts and minds through Christ Jesus.

⁸ Finally, brethren, whatsoever things are true, whatsoever things are honest, whatsoever things are just, whatsoever things are pure, whatsoever things are lovely, whatsoever things are of good report; if there be any virtue, and if there be any praise, think on these things.

DAY 20
John 13:34-35

³⁴ A new commandment I give unto you, That ye love one another; as I have loved you, that ye also love one another.

³⁵ By this shall all men know that ye are my disciples, if ye have love one to another.

DAY 21
Luke 10:25-28

²⁵ And, behold, a certain lawyer stood up, and tempted him, saying, Master, what shall I do to inherit eternal life?

²⁶ He said unto him, What is written in the law? how readest thou?

²⁷ And he answering said, Thou shalt love the Lord thy God with all thy heart, and with all thy soul, and with all thy strength, and with all thy mind; and thy neighbour as thyself.

²⁸ And he said unto him, Thou hast answered right: this do, and thou shalt live.

CHAPTER 8

STAYING MOTIVATED AND ACCOUNTABLE

Staying motivated and accountable during the Daniel Fast can be challenging, as you may encounter obstacles, setbacks, and temptations that can derail your fast. To overcome these challenges and to stay committed to your fast, you can use various strategies and resources that can help you to stay motivated and accountable.

Here are some strategies for staying motivated and accountable during the Daniel Fast:

- **Set clear and specific goals:** To stay motivated and accountable during the Daniel Fast, you can set clear and specific goals for your fast, such as losing weight, improving your health, deepening your relationship with God, or overcoming a specific challenge or addiction. By setting clear and specific goals, you can focus and direct your efforts, and you can measure and track your progress, and you can celebrate your achievements and milestones.

- **Create a plan and a schedule: To** stay motivated and accountable during the Daniel Fast, you can create a plan and a schedule for your fast that outlines your meals, your activities, your prayer and Bible study times, and your rest and relaxation times. By creating a plan and a schedule, you can prioritize and balance your commitments and responsibilities, and you can avoid overloading or underperforming, and you can manage your time and energy more efficiently and effectively.

- **Use resources and tools:** To stay motivated and accountable during the Daniel Fast, you can use resources and tools that can help you to stay on track and to overcome obstacles and temptations. Some resources and tools that you can use include a planner or a calendar, a journal or a diary, a support group or a mentor, a coach or a counselor, a recipe book or a meal plan, or a tracking app or a website. You can use these resources and tools to help you plan and prepare your meals, to monitor and record your progress, to seek and receive support and encouragement, and to overcome setbacks and challenges.

- **Enlist the support of others:** To stay motivated and accountable during the Daniel Fast, you can enlist the support of others, such as family, friends, colleagues, or a community of believers. By enlisting the support of others, you can share your journey and your experiences, and you can encourage and inspire each other, and you can hold each other accountable and responsible. You can also seek the support of

- **Take breaks and reward yourself:** To stay motivated and accountable during the Daniel Fast, you can take breaks and reward yourself for your hard work and your achievements. By taking breaks, you can give yourself a chance to rest and recharge, and you can avoid burnout and frustration. You can also reward yourself for your hard work and your achievements, by treating yourself to something that you enjoy, such as a movie, a book, a hobby, or a gift. By taking breaks and rewarding yourself, you can celebrate your success and your progress, and you can motivate yourself to continue your fast.

- **Seek accountability and accountability:** To stay motivated and accountable during the Daniel Fast, you can seek accountability and accountability from others, such as a accountability partner, a accountability group, or a accountability coach. An accountability partner is a person who you can share your goals, your challenges, and your progress with, and who can encourage and support you, and who can hold you accountable and responsible. An accountability group is a community of people who share similar goals and challenges, and who can support and encourage each other, and who can hold each other accountable and responsible. An accountability coach is a professional who can help you to set and achieve your goals, and who can provide you with guidance and feedback, and who can hold you accountable and responsible. By seeking accountability and accountability, you can receive support and encouragement, and you can stay motivated and accountable during the Daniel Fast.

Remember, the Daniel Fast is a journey, and it may have ups and downs, twists and turns, but by staying motivated and accountable, you can overcome challenges and setbacks, and you can achieve your goals and experience the benefits of the Daniel Fast.

Graham Feola

CHAPTER NINE

WRAPPING UP THE DANIEL FAST

Wrapping up the Daniel Fast can be an exciting and rewarding experience, as you can reflect on the journey and the achievements of your fast, and you can celebrate your success and your growth. By wrapping up the Daniel Fast, you can also plan and prepare for the next steps of your journey, and you can continue the momentum and the benefits of your fast, even after it is over.

Here are some ideas for wrapping up the Daniel Fast:

- **Reflect on the journey:** To wrap up the Daniel Fast, you can reflect on the journey of your fast, and you can journal or share your thoughts, your feelings, and your experiences, and you can thank God for His presence and His guidance. By reflecting on the journey, you can learn from your mistakes and your challenges, and you can appreciate your accomplishments and your blessings, and you can grow in your faith and your relationship with God.

- **Celebrate your success:** To wrap up the Daniel Fast, you can celebrate your success, and you can invite others to join you in the celebration, and you can thank God for His faithfulness and His provision. You can celebrate your success in different ways, such as by having a special meal, by giving a gift, by expressing your gratitude, by sharing your testimony, or by participating in a special activity. By celebrating your success, you can give thanks to God, and you can encourage and inspire others, and you can enjoy the fruits of your hard work and your faith.

- **Plan and prepare for the next steps:** To wrap up the Daniel Fast, you can plan and prepare for the next steps of your journey, and you can set new goals and make new commitments, and you can seek the guidance and the support of God. You can plan and prepare for the next steps by reviewing your goals and your progress, by assessing your strengths and your weaknesses, by seeking the counsel of others, and by taking small and consistent steps towards your goals. By planning and preparing for the next steps, you can stay focused and motivated, and you can continue the momentum and the benefits of the Daniel Fast, even after it is over.

- **Evaluate and adjust your habits:** To wrap up the Daniel Fast, you can evaluate and adjust your habits, and you can identify the habits that served you well during the fast, and the habits that hindered your progress or your health, and you can make changes accordingly. You can evaluate and adjust your habits by tracking your food intake, your exercise, your sleep, your stress, and your relationships, and by comparing your current habits to your goals and your values. By evaluating and adjusting your habits, you can make better and healthier choices, and you can maintain or improve your health and your well-being, and you can avoid falling back into old or unhealthy habits.

- **Seek support and accountability:** To wrap up the Daniel Fast, you can seek support and accountability, and you can surround yourself with people who can encourage and motivate you, and who can hold you accountable and responsible, and who can share your journey and your experiences. You can seek support and accountability by joining a support group or a accountability group, by finding a accountability partner or a accountability coach, by participating in a community event or a service project, or by joining a church or a ministry. By seeking support and accountability, you can avoid isolation and loneliness, and you can benefit from the wisdom and the experience of others, and you can stay motivated and accountable, even after the Daniel Fast is over.

- **Keep the fast in perspective:** To wrap up the Daniel Fast, you can keep the fast in perspective, and you can remember that the fast is a spiritual discipline, and not a magical solution or a self-improvement program, and you can avoid the temptation to rely on your own strength or your own achievements. You can keep the fast in perspective by reminding yourself of your ultimate goal and your ultimate source, and by seeking God's will and His wisdom, and by relying on His grace and His power. By keeping the fast in perspective, you can avoid pride and discouragement, and you can maintain a healthy and humble attitude, and you can continue to grow and to serve, even after the Daniel Fast is over.

Made in United States
Orlando, FL
21 February 2023

30245378R00089